UNDER PILLOW WEDDING CAKE
AND OTHER CUSTOMS
ANNOTATED
BY ALVIN FIXLER

Order this book online at www.trafford.com
or email orders@trafford.com

Most Trafford titles are also available at major online book retailers.

Note for Librarians: A cataloguing record for this book is available from Library
and Archives Canada at www.collectionscanada.ca/amicus/index-e.html

Printed in Victoria, BC, Canada.

ISBN: 978-1-4269-1455-3 (Soft)

*We at Trafford believe that it is the responsibility of us all, as both individuals
and corporations, to make choices that are environmentally and socially sound.
You, in turn, are supporting this responsible conduct each time you purchase a
Trafford book, or make use of our publishing services. To find out how you are
helping, please visit www.trafford.com/responsiblepublishing.html*

*Our mission is to efficiently provide the world's finest, most comprehensive
book publishing service, enabling every author to experience success.
To find out how to publish your book, your way, and have it available
worldwide, visit us online at www.trafford.com*

Trafford rev. 02/08/2010

 www.trafford.com

North America & international
toll-free: 1 888 232 4444 (USA & Canada)
fax: 812 355 4082 ♦ email: info@trafford.com

UNDER PILLOW WEDDING CAKE
AND OTHER CUSTOMS: ANNOTATED

PREFACE

The time frame of this book
is mainly the seventeenth and eighteenth
centuries. Seventeenth century dates
range from 1602 through 1695;eighteenth
century dates are from 1708 through 1797.
Other time periods and dates are
mentioned including 1343, 1377,1598, and
1804

Country references are mainly
England, Scotland, and Ireland;there are
also mentions of Spain and Denmark. The
material in this book was researched and
re-written from "Brand's Observations on
Popular Antiquities" by John Brand with
dates of 1888 and 1900.

A wide range of topics was utilised
to provide a broad view of the customs,
rites, beliefs, and attitudes of the
people of the aforementioned eras.These
topics include Agriculture,Animals,Birds,
Drinking, Entertainment, Foods, Holidays,
Marriage, Events, Education,Sports, and
Weather.

BOOKS BY ALVIN FIXLER:

RIVER RAFTING AND OUTDOOR
RECREATION GUIDE

LIVELY LATIN TALES

WEIRD CONTEMPORARY FABLES

. . . .

UNDER PILLOW WEDDING CAKE
AND OTHER CUSTOMS:
ANNOTATED

Preface..................I
Contents...............III
Subject Index.........VIII
Book............. 1 to 221
General Index..........222

. . . .

MONARCH AND ROYALTY PAGE REFERENCES

Charles II..81: Royal Oak Day..166:Toasts.
Duchess of York..Year:1666.40: The Montem.
Edward VI..60: Playing Cards.
Elizabeth I.3:Marriage and Betrothing
  Customs.24: New Years Day.208:Goose and
  Geese.
Henry VII.153: More Unbelievable Beliefs.
Henry VIII.28: May Day Customs I.59:
  Tavern Signs.60: PLaying Cards. 169:
  Shuffle-Board.
King William.67: Fairs.
Prince Henry Eldest Son of James I.
  111: Golf.
Prince Richard, the Son of the Black
  Prince.86: Mumming (Maskers.)
Prince of Wales.Year:1666.40.The Montem.
Prince William of Gloucester.Year: 1666
  40: The Montem.

UNDER PILLOW WEDDING CAKE
AND OTHER CUSTOMS: ANNOTATED

CONTENTS

MARRIAGE AND BETROTHING CUSTOMS.......1
ANCIENT SPORTS AND GAMES.............16
NEW YEARS EVE I......................22
NEW YEARS DAY........................23
VALENTINES DAY.......................26
MAY DAY CUSTOMS I....................27
MAY DAY CUSTOMS II...................29
MAY POLES............................30
MORRIS DANCERS.......................33
ALLHALLOW EVEN (HALLOWEEN)...........36
THE MONTEM...........................38
BAR THE SCHOOL DOORS.................42
DRINKING CUSTOMS.....................44
UNDER THE ROSE.......................52
HOB OR NOB...........................54
TAVERN SIGNS.........................56
PLAYING CARDS........................59
FAIRS................................60
FARMING AND AGRICULTURE..............69
THE FEAST OF SHEEP SHEARING..........77
THE MOON.............................78
ROYAL OAK DAY........................81
WATER CUSTOM.........................84

UNDER PILLOW WEDDING CAKE
AND OTHER CUSTOMS: ANNOTATED

CONTENTS

MUMMING (MASKERS........................85

CHRISTMAS CUSTOMS......................88

CHRISTMAS PIES.........................91

LORD OF MISRULE........................92

ANCIENT PASTIMES.......................96

BOXING................................103

CAT AND DOG...........................105

BUCKLER-PLAY..........................107

ARCHERY...............................108

GOLF..................................110

BARLEY BREAK..........................112

LOGGATS...............................113

PALL MALL.............................114

ANCIENT LOVE..........................116

FARMING CHARMS........................118

ONIONS WILL TELL......................123

MUSIC.................................125

ALL FOOLS DAY/APRIL FOOLS DAY........127

ALE...................................129

SWORD DANCE...........................130

WEATHER OMENS.........................132

AMUSING TRENCH........................135

PRESENTS FOR A GENTLEMAN'S GENTLEMAN..136

UNDER PILLOW WEDDING CAKE
AND OTHER CUSTOMS: ANNOTATED

CONTENTS

FUN WITH SAILORS...................137

"KING ARTHUR".....................139

A PRIZE OF BACON..................140

CARNIVAL TIME.....................142

FOOL PLOUGH.......................143

UNBELIEVABLE BELIEFS..............147

DARK LANTERNS.....................149

OSTRICHES.........................150

DRUIDS' EGG.......................151

MORE UNBELIEVABLE BELIEFS.........153

THE MILLER'S THUMB................155

"TO PLUCK A CROW WITH ONE".......157

TO BEAR THE BELL..................157

BULL-RUNNING......................158

ANCIENT FOOTBALL..................161

LADY OF THE LAMB..................163

TOASTS............................165

SCOTCH AND ENGLISH................167

SHUFFLE-BOARD.....................168

DRUNKARD'S CLOAK..................170

SHOES.............................171

WATCH THE ANIMALS.................172

UNDER PILLOW WEDDING CAKE
AND OTHER CUSTOMS: ANNOTATED

CONTENTS

ELECTION DAY MONDAY OCTOBER 1st 1804..177

BIG PARTY NIGHT........................181

PANCAKES..............................185

CUSHION DANCE AT WEDDINGS.............186

GOOD TIMES AT WEDDINGS................189

THE MARITAL QUESTION..................190

QUINTIN...............................191

WEDDINGS, MARRIAGES, AND SOCKS........194

SACK-POSSET...........................196

BRIDE PLACEMENT.......................197

THE HIGHGATE OATH.....................197

NEW YEARS DAY WINDS...................199

HASTY PUDDING.........................200

FISH STORY............................201

HAWTHORNE FLOWERS.....................202

MATCHMAKING...........................203

GANGING DAY...........................204

LEEKS.................................206

GOOSE AND GEESE.......................208

THE HOBBY HORSE.......................211

BRIID'S BED...........................213

SPANISH INCIDENT......................214

PUDDING PIES..........................215

UNDER PILLOW WEDDING CAKE
AND OTHER CUSTOMS: ANNOTATED

CONTENTS

STONES AND DOUGH-NUTS...............216
MAY DAY CUSTOMS III.................218
NEW YEARS EVE II....................219

UNDER PILLOW WEDDING CAKE
AND OTHER CUSTOMS: ANNOTATED

SUBJECT INDEX

AGRICULTURE

FARMING AND AGRICULTURE.................69

FARMING CHARMS........................118

THE FEAST OF SHEEP SHEARING...........77

THE MILLER'S THUMB

ANIMALS AND BIRDS

DRUID'S EGG...........................151

FISH STORY............................201

OSTRICHES.............................150

"TO PLUCK A CROW WITH ONE"............157

WATCH THE ANIMALS.....................172

DRINKING AND TAVERNS

ALE...................................129

DRINKING CUSTOMS.......................44

THE HIGHGATE OATH.....................197

HOB OR NOB.............................54

DRUNKARDS'S CLOAK.....................170

TAVERN SIGNS..........................56

TOASTS................................165

UNDER PILLOW WEDDING CAKE
AND OTHER CUSTOMS: ANNOTATED

SUBJECT INDEX

ENTERTAINMENT

BIG PARTY NIGHT.....................181
BULL RUNNING.......................158
CARNIVAL TIME......................142
FAIRS................................60
MORRIS DANCERS......................33
MUMMING.............................85
MUSIC..............................125
SWORD DANCE........................130

FOODS

HASTY PUDDING......................200
ONIONS WILL TELL...................123
PANCAKES...........................185
PUDDING PIES.......................215
STONES AND DOUGH-NUTS..............216

HOLIDAYS

ALL FOOLS DAY/APRIL FOOLS DAY.......127
ALLHALLOW EVEN......................36
CHRISTMAS CUSTOMS...................88
CHRISTMAS PIES......................91
LORD OF MISRULE.....................92

UNDER PILLOW WEDDING CAKE
AND OTHER CUSTOMS: ANNOTATED

SUBJECT INDEX

HOLIDAYS
(CONTINUED)

MAY DAY CUSTOMS I........................27

MAY DAY CUSTOMS II.......................29

MAY DAY CUSTOMS III.....................218

MAY POLES................................30

NEW YEARS DAY............................23

NEW YEARS EVE I..........................22

NEW YEARS EVE II........................219

VALENTINES DAY...........................26

MARRIAGES, WEDDINGS, AND LOVE

ANCIENT LOVE............................116

BRIDE PLACEMENT.........................197

CUSHION DANCE AT WEDDINGS...............186

GOOD TIMES AT WEDDINGS..................189

THE MARITAL QUESTION....................190

MARRIAGE AND BETROTHING CUSTOMS..........1

MATCHMAKING.............................203

A PRIZE OF BACON........................140

QUINTIN.................................191

SACK POSSET.............................196

SHOES...................................171

WEDDINGS MARRIAGES, AND SOCKS...........194

UNDER PILLOW WEDDING CAKE
AND OTHER CUSTOMS: ANNOTATED

SUBJECT INDEX

PUBLIC EVENTS

ELECTION DAY MONDAY OCTOBER 1,1804..177
FOOL PLOUGH.........................143
GANGING DAY.........................204
PALL MALL...........................114
ROYAL OAK DAY........................81

SCHOOLS AND EDUCATION

BAR THE SCHOOL DOORS.................42
THE MONTEM..........................38

SPORTS AND GAMES

ANCIENT FOOTBALL....................161
ANCIENT PASTIMES.....................96
ANCIENT SPORTS AND GAMES.............16
ARCHERY............................108
BARLEY BREAK.......................112
TO BEAR THE BELL...................157
BOXING.............................103
BUCKLER PLAY.......................107
CAT AND DOG........................105
FUN WITH SAILORS...................137
GOLF...............................110

UNDER PILLOW WEDDING CAKE
AND OTHER CUSTOMS: ANNOTATED

SUBJECT INDEX

VARIOUS SUBJECTS

AMUSING TRENCH.........................135

BRIID'S BED............................213

DARK LANTERNS..........................149

HAWTHORNE FLOWERS......................202

LEEKS..................................206

PRESENTS FOR A GENTLEMAN'S GENTLEMAN..136

THE MOON...............................78

SPANISH INCIDENT.......................214

UNBELIEVABLE BELIEFS...................147

MORE UNBELIEVABLE BELIEFS..............153

UNDER THE ROSE.........................52

WATER CUSTOM...........................84

WEATHER

NEW YEARS DAY WINDS....................199

WEATHER OMENS..........................132

UNDER PILLOW WEDDING CAKE
AND OTHER CUSTOMS: ANNOTATED

MARRIAGE AND
BETROTHING CUSTOMS

In 1794 in Scotland an annual fair was held in which single men and women looked for a friend and companion. When a man and a woman met and liked each other, they were to live together until that time next year. This custom was called "Hand-Fasting" or hand in fist. If the couple liked or hopefully loved each other by the next year, they continued together. If they didn't like or love each other, each was free to make another choice as at the first of the procedure.

What, no match-maker booth at the fair?

Why the fist? Which one had the fist?

Eighteenth century try befor you buy.

There is speculation that this fair started in Roman times when if a woman with the consent of her parents lived with a man for a year without being absent three nights she became his wife.

Three consecutive nights?

UNDER PILLOW WEDDING CAKE
AND OTHER CUSTOMS: ANNOTATED

In 1608 a betrothing ceremony was reported in which the bridegroom would cut his fingernails and send them, his pared nails, that is, to his new wife; after that they lived together as man and wife.

It's not known what she did with his finger-nails.

Cheaper than diamonds.

In ancient times it was customary for a man and a woman to break a piece of silver or gold between them; this was considered a verbal contract signifying marriage and a great deal of love. One half of the piece of silver or gold was kept by the man and one half was kept by the woman.

Was the silver or gold in the form of a wishbone?

First marital argument: who gets the bigger piece?

According to ancient Civil Law, if a couple considered marriage and the man put up money and also got a kiss, he would lose one-half of what he put up if the

(CONTINUED)..marriage didn't
happen. As far as the woman
was concerned, she could get
back whatever she gave whether
or not there was any kissing
involved if the marriage
didn't happen. That ruling,
however, only concerned
bracelets, gloves, rings, and
similar items.

Wifely privilege.

    In a tribe in a certain
country, girls had a unique
way of showing their love for
a boy. She would sit down on
a rug at the door of his hut
and give a pitcher of water to
the boy; she would then ask
him to wash his hands with the
water. After he did this she
would drink the water.

Very unique.

Hopefully no soap was used.

    During the reign of Queen
Elizabeth I, men gave their
girl friends and women gave
their boy friends small
handkerchiefs about three or

UNDER PILLOW WEDDING CAKE
AND OTHER CUSTOMS: ANNOTATED

(CONTINUED) four inches square;
the hankies were decorated
with tassels, buttons, lace,
or bright thread. The men
often wore these hankies as
tokens of their love.

Early
hanky-
panky?

In a place in 1792, if a
boy was in love with a girl
and wanted to court her,
he didn't usually go to
her father's house to see her.
He went to a Pub and told the
woman who owned the Pub the
name of his girl friend.
The woman would get in touch
with the girl and tell her to
come to the Pub, and she
usually never refused to come
there.

An early
concierge?

When the girl got to the
Pub she was greeted with ale,
whiskey, brandy, and many and
various alcoholic drinks.Then
the boy and girl got married.
The married couple invited

Did he
have to
get her
drunk to
marry her?

- 4 -

(CONTINUED) their friends to come to the Pub the second day after the marriage, and a Creeling took place. All the people then got together in a certain area.

A Creel, a basket, that is, was obtained and stones were put into it. The men ran around carrying the Creel and were chased by the women; the men soon allowed themselves to be caught by the women and when that happened the men must reward the girls with kisses.

The new husband then finally gets to run around with the basket full of stones and he must run around with it for a long time; when he does this none of the women try to chase him.

His new wife, however chases him, catches him and

This was obviously before the Hokey Pokey was invented.

The guys might have preferred a stag party.

UNDER PILLOW WEDDING CAKE
AND OTHER CUSTOMS: ANNOTATED

(CONTINUED) takes the basket full of stones from him. This is an indication that she is very happy about marrying her husband and loves him very much. The basket goes around again for more running around and everybody has a good time. Later they all get together, have dinner, and talk about their exciting and thrilling basket-carrying activities.

Good girl! An indication of a happy future marriage. If she sees him running around carrying a basket of stones later, she will certainly help him again.

Many years ago a story was related that on the day before a Duke and a Princess were to be married a large pile of potsherds (fragments of pottery) was formed in front of the door of the abode of the Princess.

Unusual front yard decoł.

People would then pick up the pieces and throw them against the door with a great deal of force. While this was going on the Princess would

We prefer to throw rice, thank you.

(CONTINUED) peek out of the door. This custom is also said to be performed in a European country on the day before a virgin is married.

She probably wanted a look at her well-wishers.

The wedding cake also anciently called the bride-cake is one of the most important parts of a marriage. Many years ago in a European country the cake was cut into small square pieces and then thrown over the bride and the bridegroom's head.

Before, after, or while the bride and groom fed each other the cake?

At other times the cake was broken over the bride's head, and then thrown out to the crowd who scrambled for the pieces. Another custom was for young and single people to put pieces of the cake under their respective pillows at night hoping to dream of their future mates and lovers.

Bouquet throwing was more pleasant and less messy.

Sounds somewhat like a Tooth Fairy variation.

Among the Romans a bride

UNDER PILLOW WEDDING CAKE
AND OTHER CUSTOMS: ANNOTATED

(CONTINUED) was prepared for marriage in the following way: A chaplet (garland or wreath) of flowers or herbs was put on her head and she wore a girdle of sheep's wool around her middle. The girdle was tied with a true-loves-knot which her husband was to untie and unfasten. This was a symbol that he had undone what people called her "Virgin's Girdle," meaning that he had made her a woman.

Warm and toasty.

No fumbling allowed.

Things were simpler then.

Gloves were often given at marriages in ancient times. One of these customs involved a clergyman asking the groom if a pair of red gloves with three pieces of silver money was readily available.

Wedding planners and consultants had to think of everything.

If they had them there, the gloves were put into the groom's right hand; when his hand was joined with the

UNDER PILLOW WEDDING CAKE
AND OTHER CUSTOMS: ANNOTATED

(CONTINUED) bride's hand, the gloves were left on her hand. Garters were considered prize possessions at weddings in certain countries. Men would go after the bride in order to pluck the garter off of her leg immediately after the ceremony and right in front of the altar.

Who got the money?

Male attendance at weddings was probably quite high.

This procedure often turned into what might be considered somewhat of a riotous contest, and the bride often ended up on the floor. The man who managed to get the garter displayed it around the church triumphantly.

Neither lady-like nor bride-like.

The situation got to the point where the bride was almost being assaulted and a solution had to be found to protect her. Some one suggested that the bride give garters out of her bosom.

A doubtful solution to say the least.

- 9 -

(CONTINUED) There are no known
reports as to whether or not
this suggestion was adopted.
It may have then been decided
that the bride was better off
ending up on the floor.
According to other reports
contending for the garters
took place after the bride had
been put to bed.

On your
mark..get
set..go
get the
garter.

Another version of this
situation says that when bed
time came around, contenders
for the garters would pull off
the bride's garters which she
had previously loosened   so
that they might hang down.

Try, try,
again.

The reason for this was
to prevent some one's   hand
from getting too familiar
while searching   for   the
garter. After that the garters
were fastened to the hats of
the men, and the bridesmaids
would carry the bride into the

But, of
course
they were
all
gentlemen.

UNDER PILLOW WEDDING CAKE
AND OTHER CUSTOMS: ANNOTATED

(CONTINUED) bride chamber and
put her to bed. There also
was music at weddings and a   Musical
piper always had a piece of   inspiration
the bride's garter tied about
his pipes.

     Kissing goes on a lot
during weddings and years
ago during the dancing if a
violin player thinks there's
been enough music he will   We tap
play two notes on his   glasses
                                   now.
instrument which were
interpreted to mean: "Kiss
Her!."

     In 1793 in some places
just before a marriage
ceremony, every knot on the   Fashion
clothes of the bride and   gurus take
                                   note: the
groom was loosened. The items   latest
involved included shoe   casual
                                   look.
strings; garters; dresses;
petticoats; shirts; vests;
pants, sashes; scarves;coats;
etc.; etc.

(CONTINUED) After leaving the church every one would walk around it keeping the church walls always upon the right hand.The Bridegroom,however, first retires one way with some young men to tie the knots that were loosened about him, while the young married woman, in the same manner, retires somewhere else to adjust the disorder of her Dress.

Any volunteers to help her?

Brides used to sell ale during the wedding day, charging good prices for each pint to friends, relatives, guests, and visitors. The reason was simple: the money she made helped defray the cost of the wedding dinner.It was also customary for people to make contributions to the bride and bridegroom; this was not only a sign of

Maybe a free kiss with each pint?

UNDER PILLOW WEDDING CAKE
AND OTHER CUSTOMS: ANNOTATED

(CONTINUED) philanthropy but also helped increase the population by encouraging people to get married. Many years ago an event called a Penny Bridal was performed. When a man and a woman were contracted to be married they would go to a local tavern to announce their engagement.

Ater that they would travel all over the area for miles around in every direction looking for and inviting guests to their wedding.

They sometimes collected as much as three hundred people who would then go to that aforementioned tavern to drink, party, and have a great good time at their ----the guests----expense, not the bridegroom and brides.

Get hitched and get rich was the motto.

A B.Y.O.C. --Bring Your Own Cash-- party.

- 13 -

UNDER PILLOW WEDDING CAKE
AND OTHER CUSTOMS: ANNOTATED

In 1721 after a wedding friends would sometimes go to the married couple's house and go into the bedroom while the newlyweds were still in bed. The friends would be bringing wedding presents and they would throw the presents on top of the bedclothes under which the couple were lying. According to reports, these presents often consisted of household furniture.

Hopefully no sectional sofas.

One of the more amusing marriage customs was to hang a bell under the bride and bridegroom's bed.

Post wedding activities often went on the morning after the marriage. Sometimes all the people who had attended the ceremony the night before would troop into the bedroom of the newlyweds

Follow the leader.

(CONTINUED) before they arose. Then, after the couple woke up they would listen to the husband declare the morning gift which was usually a garment or cloak with a veil for his wife. Another practice was to awaken the newlyweds early in the morning with a concert of music.

Husband: "Get those people and that music out of here"

The ancient name for the marriage ceremony was confarreation, and the token of the solemn union between a man and a woman was a cake of wheat or barley.

Sometimes the couple ate a cake of salt, water, and flour. When the bride came home from church, wheat was often thrown on her head, and when the bride and groom got home they were presented with a pot of butter. The butter

Yummy, yummy.

We throw rice.

UNDER PILLOW WEDDING CAKE
AND OTHER CUSTOMS: ANNOTATED

(CONTINUED) was a wish for plenty of food and lots of all good things.

ANCIENT SPORTS AND GAMES

Football was considered a useful and charming exercise in the winter. The ball itself was described as a leather ball filled with air about as big as a person's head. It was kicked about from one person to another in the streets of a city.

Not exactly adaptable for a forward pass.

Much simpler than now.

No flags going down.

That was the whole game.

The exact time this version of football started is hard to determine, but it appears to have been popular in the reign of Edward III of England.

There was a problem with this sport however; the popularity of football interfered with the practice

(CONTINUED)of archery, so it, football, was prohibited by a public edict in the thirty-nineth year of that monarch's reign.

A game called Handy Dandy was described as being played in three different ways. One of the methods was to have a player hold up his fingers to signify a certain number. Right after that he would move his fingers up and down so that his opponent couldn't read the number he is showing.

How's that again?

A second version was called a children's game where the kids change hands and places where they sit. A third version describes the game as being played by putting an object in one or another hand and then putting the two hands together and shaking them at the same time.

Musical chairs?

(CONTINUED) The goal was for
the other players to guess in
which hand the object is
finally deposited.

Any bets taken?

Meritot was a sport
enjoyed by both children and
adults where the individual
swung himself or herself at
the end of ropes until he or
she became dizzy. It was
called Shuggy-Shew in th
north of England. Adults of
the higher classes engaged in
this sport at places where
they could get drinks.

Also known as hang-out joints.

A game called Nine Men's
Morris or Merrils was played
in a certain part of England.
Shepherds, farmers and other
youths would go to a certain
area and dig up the turf with
their knives.

They would then make a
square which ranged from a
foot square to three or four

(CONTINUED) yards square;this
was expanded to make a rough
chessboard.Two groups of nine
men each were then formed;one
group had wooden pegs and the
other group had stones.
The opposing groups would
move their wooden pegs and
stones to try to "capture" Not
their opponents. An area exactly
quite
inside the "chessboard" was like
called the pound in which men chess.
"captured" were kept.

Horse races were very
popular among the English
nobility many years ago.
Distinguished and wealthy
gentlemen used to go to a
certain famous track and bet
as much as two thousand
pounds on a race. A traveller
passing through the area and
stopping at the track
reported something quite
interesting: Some of the races

UNDER PILLOW WEDDING CAKE
AND OTHER CUSTOMS: ANNOTATED

(CONTINUED) were also run by men.

Same tote board?

During the end of the eighteenth century a popular game or sport called Diversion of the Ring or Riding at the Ring was played in Europe. It was created by people who thought there was too much drinking at social gatherings and the people would be better off engaged in sports with no drinking allowed.

In whose opinion?

It was a sport of both ancient and warlike origin. Two posts were erected and a cross-beam was put at the top from which a small ring was suspended.Player/competitors rode horseback carrying pointed rods; the goal of the sport was to ride at full gallop and carry of on the rod.

It would be more fun if drinking was allowed.

UNDER PILLOW WEDDING CAKE
AND OTHER CUSTOMS: ANNOTATED

Playing with a top anciently known as Whipping the Top or Whirligig was mentioned in both Greek and Latin literature. Illuminated manuscripts of the fourteenth century show boys playing with tops. Young people were advised to play with tops rather than shoot dice.

Has Las Vegas heard about this?

The expression "sleep like a top" came about because the top was said to sleep while turning around very fast and also making a smooth humming sound. At one time almost every village had a large top that the inhabitants would go out and whip, play with, that is, in cold, frosty weather. The reason for this was so that the peasants would keep warm from the exercise and keep out of mischief when they were unable to work.

Or so they were told.

UNDER PILLOW WEDDING CAKE
AND OTHER CUSTOMS: ANNOTATED

NEW YEARS EVE I

Anciently, the popular word on New Years Eve was Wassail and Wassail Bowl. Young women went around with a bowl of that name filled with spiced ale from door to door of houses. Please girls, no sampling.

While they walked they sang songs and accepted presents from the people in the various places where they stopped to wish Happy New Year greetings. The meaning of the word "Wassail" is derived from the Anglo-Saxon phrase " Be in Health."

In 1784 another drinking custom was for the master of the house to fill a large bowl or pitcher, drink out of it himself, and then give it to the person next to him. That individual would take a swig First master swig, of course.

UNDER PILLOW WEDDING CAKE
AND OTHER CUSTOMS: ANNOTATED

(CONTINUED) and then pass it
to the next person, and on
and on and the bowl went
around.

Anything
left at
the end?

NEW YEARS DAY

People many years ago
believed in ending the old
year well and making a good
beginning of the new one. As
now, New Years Eve was the
time of singing, dancing,
partying, and of course, the
Wassail Bowl.

Kissing
and
confetti,
too.

On New Years Day
the popular word was somewhat
different: Presents. People
sent gifts to friends and
acquaintances to celebrate
the New Year. All of these
customs--New Years Eve and
New Years Day-were observed
with the hope that the coming
year would be prosperous,
happy, successful, and of
good cheer for every one.

The
retailers
liked
this.

UNDER PILLOW WEDDING CAKE
AND OTHER CUSTOMS: ANNOTATED

(CONTINUED) An orange stuck with cloves was a favorite New Year gift; rosemary and nutmeg were also used to enhance the New Year with pleasant aromas and thoughts.

Unusual to say the least.

Pins were acceptable New Year gifts to women, and they used them to fasten drapery instead of the wooden skewers which were used until the end of the fifteenth century. Sometimes they received money instead of the pins.

We still use the term "pin money."

On New Years Day Queen Elizabeth I received all kinds of monetary gifts and various items from many people including high ranking individuals, bishops, friends, and various chief officers of the government.

She also received gifts from the palace household servants such as the master

(CONTINUED) cook and the serjeant of the pastry. Besides monetary gifts, Elizabeth received jewelry; trinkets; rich gowns; petticoats; shifts; silk stockings; garters; doublets; mantles embroidered with precious stones; furs; bracelets; and looking glasses.

Cookies, maybe.

All those palace closets really came in handy.

Her physician gave her a box of foreign confectionery; she also received a pot of green ginger and one of orange flowers. Her pharmacists gave her pots of lozenges, ginger candy and other conserves.

Right from the drug store.

A Mrs.Morgan contributed a box of cherries and a box of apricots.Mrs.Blanche Parry gave Elizabeth a little gold comfit-box and spoon.A cutler (knife dealer) presented a

Chocolate covered?

UNDER PILLOW WEDDING CAKE
AND OTHER CUSTOMS: ANNOTATED

(CONTINUED)meat-knife to Her
Majesty; Smyth, a servant
gave her two bolts of cambric
(A fine white linen).On the
basis of some reports, she
did return some of the gifts.

VALENTINE"S DAY

A Valentine ceremony long
ago consisted of putting the
names of a certain number of
one sex--say,males--into a
pot or glass vessel; then the
names of females are put
into another vessel.

Saved
matchmaker
fees.

After   that   there's   a
drawing: the men draw from
the woman's vessel and the
women draw from the men's
vessel. The names that are
drawn are called Valentines
and the match-ups between men
and women were looked upon as
a good omen of their becoming
man and wife in the future.

Romantic
raffle
or
sweet
sweepstakes.

(CONTINUED) Another Valentine saying or custom concerned the following: If a man is walking on a street on the fourteenth of February, the first woman he sees is his Valentine; if a woman is walking on a street on that date the first man she sees is her Valentine.

Hi.
Hi.
As simple as that.

MAY DAY CUSTOMS I

A little after midnight on the morning on the morning of May first, the boys and girls in villages in the north of England would run to the woods accompanied by a lot of music and horns.

What did the neighbors say?

There they broke branches down from trees and decorated them with nosegays and crowns of flowers. After this, around sunrise they returned to their homes and decorated the doors and

UNDER PILLOW WEDDING CAKE
AND OTHER CUSTOMS: ANNOTATED

(CONTINUED) windows with the
flowery branches. The use of
horns was prevalent on the
first of May with people
blowing them and drinking out   At the
of them.   same time?

It is on record that King
Henry VIII and Queen Katherine
and their courtiers rose up
early on May day and went to
the woods. There they got
green branches from the trees
and after that the King and
Queen went shooting in the
wood with their bows and
arrows.

On the first of May and
the five or six days following
all the pretty young country
girls who brought milk to
towns would dress up and put   Flowers
flowers on their heads instead   felt
of milk-pails.   better.

They would then,
accompanied by bagpipe or

- 28 -

UNDER PILLOW WEDDING CAKE
AND OTHER CUSTOMS: ANNOTATED

(CONTINUED) fiddle, go from
door to door dancing before
the houses of their customers.
Boys and girls would follow
them in troops and every one
gave the milk-maids and boys
and girls something.

MAY DAY CUSTOMS II

A report in the "Morning Post"
newspaper of May 2, 1791 said
that on the day before, which
was May Day, people went into
the fields and bathed their
faces with the dew on the
grass. They did this because,
according to custom, this
procedure would make them
beautiful.

Idea for
cosmetic
companies:
bottle it
and
sell
it.

Young chimney-sweepers
celebrated May Day in London
by dressing up in a lovely
and attractive way: They
covered themselves with brick
dust, paint, and gilt paper.
They also went around making a

Let's just
say
"unusual
way."

(CONTINUED) great deal of noise with their shovels and brushes.

Marriage customs were sometimes combined with May Day. A May Feast was prepared by putting warm cow's milk, sweet cake, and wine in a container like a pot. A wedding ring was dropped into that mixture and various individuals would fish for that ring with a ladle. This was a way of trying to find out who shall be first to get married.

Gourmet special.

Pre-game before the marriage game.

MAY POLES

In ancient times people held what they called an anniversary assembly on May Day and the May Pole was considered the great standard of justice. The Pole was usually in the area known as the Commons or Fields of May.

Cheaper than a court house.

UNDER PILLOW WEDDING CAKE
AND OTHER CUSTOMS: ANNOTATED

(CONTINUED)The people at this place got rid of or punished their governors, kings, or barons in cases of corruption or crimes.Symbols of authority including the judge's bough or wand; the staff, rod, and mace of civil power; and the truncheon of the military field officers are all derived from May Day and May Pole procedures at that time.

Gavel too, maybe?

A Mayor received his title of lawful power during this May time period. The crown, a mark of dignity, and symbol of power, like the mace and the sceptre was also taken from the May. All these were representative of the garland or crown which when hung on the top of the May Pole was the great signal for convening the people.

His honor was honored.

Less noise than a bell.

May Day was considered

UNDER PILLOW WEDDING CAKE
AND OTHER CUSTOMS: ANNOTATED

(CONTINUED) the boundary day
between winter and summer.
This concept was turned
into a sport and two troops of
youths were organized: one of
the troops dressed in winter
clothes, and the other troop
dressed in summer clothes.

Friendly
uniform
rivalry.

After that there was a
mock "war" between the two
groups with the winter troop
"fighting" in defence of the
continuance of winter,and the
other group trying to bring
in the summer.

No
real
violence,
of course.

The summer troop always
won the "battle" which they
happily and joyously
celebrated by triumphantly
carrying green branches wit
May flowers around the area
and singing songs like "We
have brought the summer home!"

A
warm
victory.

In Ireland in 1682 on May
Eve many families put a green

(CONTINUED) bush covered with yellow flowers on the doors of their homes. If they lived in areas where there was plenty of timber,people would cut down tall, high and slender trees and put them in front of their houses.

A nice welcome.

This would give their houses a somewhat familiar look;   thirsty   strangers wandering around would think that   these   places   were ale-sellers and that all these houses were taverns.

Sorry, no drinks here; just families.

MORRIS DANCERS

Morris Dancing was an activity carried on in England at various times during the fifteenth,   sixteenth, seventeenth, and eighteenth centuries.

The origin is ascribed to the Moors in Spain.

Robin Hood and the celebration of May were both involved with Morris Dancing.

UNDER PILLOW WEDDING CAKE
AND OTHER CUSTOMS: ANNOTATED

(CONTINUED) It was said that
the introduction of Robin Hood
into the celebration of May
suggested the addition of a
King or lord of May. Many of
the Morris Dancers portrayed
characters from the Robin Hood
stories.

A merry time for the Merry Men.

    Friar Tuck, Will Scarlet,
Stokesley, and Little John
were mentioned. Maid Marion
was often Queen of the May and
played a prominent role in
plays and celebrations.

Maid Marion was Robin's sweetheart.

    The name Robin Hood is
of course synonymmous with
bows and arrows and the May
Games of Robin Hood were
instituted   for   the
encouragement of archery.

Dancers: mind those arrows.

    Those Games were usually
accompanied by Morris Dancers.

    One of the real
characters in the Morris
group had the name of Tom the

(CONTINUED) Piper.He was sent
around the country to make
collections.He was a colorful
individual with his tabor (a
small drum,) tabor-stick, and
pipe. There was a feather in
his cap and he carried a
sword and what looked like a
shield.

Many people looked at
him and thought he was a
squire minstrel or a minstrel
of the superior order. Tom
Piper's hat was red, faced or
turned up with yellow; his
doublet was blue and the
sleeves blue turned up with
yellow.

Dressed
like this
he would
certainly
need
to
carry
a
sword.

There was some kind of
red covering on his wrists.
Over his doublet was a red
garment like a short cloak
with arm holes; his cape was
yellow and his hose red.

Garnished across   and

UNDER PILLOW WEDDING CAKE
AND OTHER CUSTOMS: ANNOTATED

(CONTINUED) perpendicularly on his thighs there was narrow yellow lace. His shoes were brown.

Tom Piper: "Pay me and I'll go away."

ALLHALLOW EVEN

On Halloween, young people in the North of England used to dive for apples in a very unique way: The apples were stuck on one end of a kind of hanging beam, with a lighted candle on the other end of the beam.

Slightly more of a challenge than modern day bobbing.

The individual had to get the apple with his or her mouth with their hands tied behind their backs. A variation of this techniqu was when a person balanced himself or herself upon a pole laid across two stools.

At the end of the pole is a lighted candle from which the person is trying to light another candle at the

(CONTINUED) risk of tumbling into a tub of water placed under him.

Nuts and apples were very popular on Halloween, and many people liked to throw the nuts into the fire, or cracked them open with their teeth. This is how that night got the name of "Nutcracker Night."

Dentists, take note.

On the subject of nuts, during ancient Roman marriage ceremonies, the bridegroom threw nuts about a room for the boys to scramble and get.

He'll be busy with other diversions.

It was a token that the party throwing and scattering the nuts was now leaving childish diversions.Regarding nuts again, on the first of November, which was near Halloween,people in rural areas would throw nuts in fires to see what would

UNDER PILLOW WEDDING CAKE
AND OTHER CUSTOMS: ANNOTATED

(CONTINUED) happen. This practice concerned matrimonial matters. If the nuts stayed still and burned happily together, it meant a happy marriage or a hopeful love; if the nuts bounced around and flew all over the area, it was not considered a good sign for the marriage.

One is tempted to make certain possible comparisons.

Another Halloween custom described in a Welsh Dictionary involved boys and girls running among ash trees looking for an even-leaved sprig. If a boy found one, he would call out the word "Cyniver;"if a girl finds one at exactly the same time, it was said that this was an omen that that boy and girl would be married.

The girl, at least knew what that word meant.

THE MONTEM

According to historical records, The Montem was a

UNDER PILLOW WEDDING CAKE
AND OTHER CUSTOMS: ANNOTATED

(CONTINUED) ceremony,actually
a procession or parade, that
took place at a prominent
English school. According to
an ancient publication dated
1666, the head of a college
extolled the glories of salt
as part of higher education.

Also, incidently can be put on food.

He called salt the
emblem of wisdom and learning
not only on account of its
composition, but also on its
uses. He said salt consisted
of the purest matter, and so
also wisdom should be pure,
sound, immaculate, and
incorruptible.

Salt manufacturers, take note: new promotion idea.

So the aforementioned
school had a parade involving
salt. The parade was like
many other processions except
for one feature: People
walking in the parade asked
for donations of money from
the watchers and spectators

This was the Montem.

UNDER PILLOW WEDDING CAKE
AND OTHER CUSTOMS: ANNOTATED

(CONTINUED) and the donors were
rewarded with.......salt. A
description of one of these
Montems dated June, 1793 is
as follows:The students of the
college assembled in the
school-yard and were properly
lined up according to their
rank in school.

Will receiving the salt affect the donor's tax situation?

Their Majesties, with the
Prince of Wales, Princesses
Royal, Augusta, Elizabeth,
and Emilia; the Duchess of
York; and Prince William of
Gloucester arrived at the
college.

Royal guests, too. Very impressive.

The royal guests took
their viewing places in the
stable-yard. The students
marched twice around the
school yard, and then went in
true military style, with
music playing, drums beating,
and colors flying, into the
stable-yard.

Bleachers or grand-stand?

UNDER PILLOW WEDDING CAKE
AND OTHER CUSTOMS: ANNOTATED

(CONTINUED) They marched past
the royal guests and dipped
the flag to their majesties.
The procession then moved on
through the playing fields to
Salt Hill, where they were
again received by the royal
entourage.

A salute
to
royalty

Well
named.

The students marched by
and again saluted the royal
group, and then marched off
to dinner. Five hundred
students marched in this
procession. The money the
students collected, for which
they gave out salt, amounted
to one thousand pounds.

Nice
take,but
what did
the salt
cost?

Their Royal Majesties;
the Prince of Wales; the
Princesses; and the Duchess
of York all made their
donations to the Salt-Bearers.
In the evening the students
returned and afterwards the
Salt-Bearers appeared on the

And got
you-
know-
what in
return.

(CONTINUED) terrace and were particularly noticed by their Royal Majesties who duly acknowledged the important function of all the Salt-Bearers.

Nice job, and the palace shakers are full.

BAR THE SCHOOL DOORS

An interesting practice, if that's what it could be called, took place at a number of colleges in the seventeenth and eighteenth centuries.

In 1683 in England, the students "barred-out" the Master of a school. This happened at the approach of the usual time when the students are dismissed and the school closes for vacation.

Not very respectful to say the least.

The kids don't want to wait for the time of the formal dismissal, so they close and lock the door and

UNDER PILLOW WEDDING CAKE
AND OTHER CUSTOMS: ANNOTATED

(CONTINUED) refuse to let the
Master in. They also verbally
defy the Master from the
windows. They do probably
eventually let him him.

Called higher education.

At another college, in
September or October the
Master is locked out of the
school and before he can get
back in he must tell the
students about the different
holidays for the upcoming
year,and must promise to
observe those holidays.

He must also sign his
name to what are called
"Orders" describing those
promises. The "Orders" must be
signed in the presence of two
Bondsmen.(Notaries?)

Of course we trust you, but sign anyway.

When he does this, it's
a signal that he has given in
to the students. After that
the doors are opened, the
Master is admitted, and

UNDER PILLOW WEDDING CAKE
AND OTHER CUSTOMS: ANNOTATED

(CONTINUED) every one gets
together for a lavish banquet
of beef, beer, and wine. They
all spend the rest of the day
laughing and kidding around.
This practice of barring th
Master out of school was
obviously a permitted and
tolerated "prank."

All is
forgiven
kids! Let's
whoop
it up!

A
curriculum
goodie.

DRINKING CUSTOMS

The word "pledge" has a
number of meanings and also
connotations. It can mean a
sign or token of something;
an item left as security; a
solemn and serious promise;
and a term related   to
drinking, such as drinking to
a person's health.

Also called
a toast.

In ancient times, people,
especially men, carried
swords, knives, or daggers.
When invaders ruled certain
countries, they, the invaders,
had a nasty habit of stabbing

UNDER PILLOW WEDDING CAKE
AND OTHER CUSTOMS: ANNOTATED

(CONTINUED) the inhabitants
in the act of drinking. This
didn't happen all the time,
but often enough to be a
serious situation. So the
inhabitants came up with what
may be called a temporary
solution.

Also
very
unsoc-
iable.

For example, if two men
friends went into a bar for a
drink and one of them was
afraid of being stabbed while
downing a pint of ale, he
would ask his friend to
"pledge" him. This meant that
the friend would, in effect
guard him and see to it that
he doesn't get a knife or
dagger thrust into his anatomy.

Watch for
a
glint of
steel.

Another version of the
meaning of the word "pledge"
regarding drinking concerns a
person to whom others drink to,
such as a toast; if the person
toasted doesn't drink, he or

- 45 -

UNDER PILLOW WEDDING CAKE
AND OTHER CUSTOMS: ANNOTATED

(CONTINUED) she could find another as a pledge to receive the drink. In this way the individual proposed to would still receive the honor.

Volunteers: please line up.

A drinking custom called pin drinking and also called nick the pin was popular in England many years ago. Pins or nails would be installed on the inside of drinking cups or horns.

Sharp ones.

Bets were made, and the individual who could drink exactly to the pin in a cup, neither under it nor over it would win the wager.

Gambling chuck-a lug.

A 1647 paper from England describes a man who was called a "good fellow" and also a "goad fellow." The "goad fellow" appellation concerned him trying to force and goad his fellow drinkers to continue to drink until

"When I drink, every one drinks"

UNDER PILLOW WEDDING CAKE
AND OTHER CUSTOMS: ANNOTATED

(CONTINUED) they got drunk.
He did this by constantly
saying "Pray pledge me" and
if they didn't keep
drinking he would say that
they dishonored and disgraced
him. (Another meaning and
connotation of the word
"pledge" meant "Have a
drink with me.")

An insistent type, to say the least

A 1619 Irish publication
described a mode of
drinking to some one's health.
A man in a public house would
first take off his cap, then
take a full cup of an
alcoholic beverage in his
hand.

Next he would look very
seriously at his audience.
Every one would quiet down
and there was absolute
silence in the place, as he
looked at each person.

Attention please.

Tbe people in the

(CONTINUED) place waited
in expectation as to what he
was going to do. The man would
then mention the name of, and
drink to the health of, a
well known individual in the
audience who may definitely
and absolutely not want to be
recognized as being in that
place at that time.

That famous personage
must, however,stand, take off
his cap, kiss his fingers,
and bow in reverent acceptance
of the toast to his health.

"I'm glad
cameras
are not
invented
yet"

The year was 1617, and
the place was England. Six men
determined to test their
strengths with regard to see
who could drink the most
glasses of an alcoholic
beverage.

A
real
challenge.

The first individual
drank one pint; the second
person, two pints; the third

(CONTINUED) drank three pints;
the fourth, four pints; the
fifth , five pints; and the
sixth, six pints.

The round starts again,
and one more pint is added to
each individual. The first
one drinks seven pints; the
second drinks eight pints;
the third, nine pints; the
fourth, ten pints; the fifth,
eleven pints; and the sixth,
twelve pints.

Better call the distributor.

Adding up all the pints
consumed comes to: the first
person, eight pints; the
second, ten pints; the third,
twelve pints; the fourth,
fourteen pints; the fifth,
sixteen pints; and the sixth,
eighteen pints.

Should make the Middle Ages Book of Records.

The official report of
this remarkable, to say the
least, drinking encounter
ends here.

(CONTINUED) Many years ago there was a club of drinkers who called themselves "Facers," and it was said that they would rather spend a large amount of money for ale than a small amount for meat.

They got their name from a strict rule they observed: If they drank a cup of ale and left some in the cup, they threw what was left in their own faces. Therefore, in order to save their faces and clothes, they always drank their cups dry.

Some rules are made to be necessarily broken.

A Scotch publication dated 1791 described an interesting and kind custom involving people who have losses or misfortunes of any kind, including financial problems.

When this happened to an individual, a friend would go

(CONTINUED) around to many of
his neighbors and invite them
to what they called a
"Drinking" at his, the
unfortunate person's, house.

Y'all
come.

    This "Drinking" session
consisted of a little small
Beer, with a bit of bread and
cheese, and sometimes a small
glass of Brandy or Whiskey.
The Brandy or Whiskey was
previously provided by the
needy person or his friend.

A "wee"
beer.

    The guests convened at
the appointed time and after
collecting a shilling apiece,
and sometimes more, they had
a good time for a couple of
hours with Music and Dancing.
After that, the participants
went home.

A
wonder-
ful
example
of
Scotch
caring
and
charity.

    If a person couldn't
attend the "Drinking," they
usually sent their money with
a neighbor that did attend.

UNDER PILLOW WEDDING CAKE
AND OTHER CUSTOMS: ANNOTATED

(CONTINUED) These parties
sometimes produced five, six,
and seven pounds for the
needy person or family.

UNDER THE ROSE

According to ancient
beliefs and historians, the
rose was the symbol of
silence. Some writers say that
the rose was the flower of
Venus, which Cupid consecrated
to Harpocrates, the god of
silence; the flower was
therefore made the emblem for
concealment of the mysteries
of Venus.

Roses and
Love also
go
together.

It was once the fashion
to stick a rose in the ear;
the first Lord North had a
juvenile portrait (supposed to
be that of Queen Elizabeth I)
representing this fashion.

Obvious
symbol:
the ear,
silence.

During the Wars of the
Roses in England (1455-1485)

(CONTINUED) the Red Rose was one of several badges of the House of Lancaster, and the White Rose was the badge of Richard, Duke of York.

Whenever either faction had a meeting or conference, an individual would say to his friend concerning the subject talked about that he "said it under the rose."

Hopefully there were no bugs of any kind in any roses in the room.

This meant that whatever was said during the meeting was to be kept absolutely secret and confidential.

What is described as a common country custom involved people gathered at a house for a party, feast, or banquet. After eating and drinking and talking and having a good time, it was agreed by all present that all the talk in that room was not to leave the room.

Not even juicy gossip?

(CONTINUED)Therefore the
phrase that was used was
that everything was spoken
"under the rose." Roses were
hung over tables in parlors
and dining rooms to remind
people of keeping all talk
and conversations strictly
confidential. A publication
dated 1638 described how
many places in England and
Low Countries had a rose
painted over tables for the
same reasons of vocal
security.

Mum's the word could be said except that these are roses.

HOB OR NOB

There are a number of
interpretations and
explanations with regard to
the expression "Hob or Nob."
Some may be true, some not
true, and some possibly
folklore.

If an individual went
into a restaurant or tavern

(CONTINUED) and saw a friend there, he might say to the friend: "Will you Hob or Nob with me?" This was a request or challenge to drink a glass of wine with the proposer; if the challenged individual answered "Nob" the two were to decide between white or red.

Why a challenge which implies a duel or defiance?

Another intriguing explanation, which some scholars doubt, concerns the North Country (England) name for the back of the chimney which is "Hob" or "Hub."

The following is said to have originated in the days of Good Queen Bess: Great and huge chimneys were in fashion at that time.

Fireplaces too?
Lots of stockings for Santa.

Inside the house, and at each corner of the hearth or grate there was a small elevated projection called

UNDER PILLOW WEDDING CAKE
AND OTHER CUSTOMS: ANNOTATED

(CONTINUED)the "Hob" and behind it a seat. In the winter,beer was placed on the "Hob" to warm. Cold beer was set on a small table said to have been called the "Nob."

Was the seat warm too?

Better,even in the winter.

If a person was thirsty they would be asked: "Will you have "Hob" or "Nob?" meaning will you have warm or cold beer, that is,beer from the "Hob" or "Nob?"

"Neither. just a shot of Scotch, please."

TAVERN SIGNS

A June, 1793 publication had an article to the effect that in the reign of Phillip and Mary the Earl of Arundel acquired the right to license public houses.

Licenses were precious then as now.

Part of the armorial design of the family was a checkered board, so owners of ale-houses and taverns used that design as part of their

UNDER PILLOW WEDDING CAKE
AND OTHER CUSTOMS: ANNOTATED

(CONTINUED) signs; they did
this to show that they were
licensed. In September, 1794
the same publication had an
article saying that the
checkered design represented
the coat-of-arms of the Earls
of Warenne and Surrey, and in
the reign of Edward IV,they,
the aforementioned Earls,had
the right to license public
houses.

Sounds like modern times.

Solution? simple: the pubs had to pay for two licenses if there was a cost.

Another reason for that
particular design was that in
the Middle Ages financial
and money matters were
arranged by merchants,
accountants, and judges on
tables called exchequers from
their resemblance to chess
boards.

A sign in front of a
building showing a
checkerboard meant that there
was a money changer inside;

UNDER PILLOW WEDDING CAKE
AND OTHER CUSTOMS: ANNOTATED

(CONTINUED) later on the sign
came to indicate an ale-house,
tavern, inn, or house of
entertainment. The previously
mentioned armorial design and
coat-of-arms of the Earls
were also certainly a factor
regarding the looks of the
signs.

> They better have a license.

Putting everything
together, the fact was that
the owner of the tavern or
inn also engaged in money
changing and other financial
matters. Another theory about
the checkerboard design of
the signs concerned the
playin of games such as
draughts (checkers) in public
houses and taverns.

> What? No banks or ATMs?

> No darts yet?

There were, of course,
other designs and devices on
tavern signs. The name of one
tavern was the "Bull and Gate"
and this name was derived from

(CONTINUED) the Boulogne Gates
which Henry VIII ordered to
be removed and transported to
Hardes in Kent. Boulogne Mouth
was the entry to the harbor
of Boulogne after it was
captured in 1544; the tavern
name became the "Bull and
Mouth." A black bull with a
huge mouth was pictured on
the sign.

Stretched
a little,
but close
enough.

Terrific
neon sign
if they
had neon
then.

PLAYING CARDS

Card games were, to a
certain extent, prohibited by
law in the eleventh year of
the reign of Henry VII.
However, they were very
generally played by people
anyway; games were allowed
during the Christmas holidays
for certain people, and then
only in private homes.

Laughably
unenfor-
cible.

Ironically, and in spite
of the law, cards were a

UNDER PILLOW WEDDING CAKE
AND OTHER CUSTOMS: ANNOTATED

(CONTINUED) highly fashionable court amusement during the reign of Henry VII. An account of money disbursed for his use shows an entry of one hundred shillings having been paid to him at one time for the purpose of playing at cards.

Poker? Rummy any one? And you better let me win.

Nice stake but did he have to re-pay the money if he won?

Henry VIII, however, preferred field sports rather than sedentary amusements. Sir William Forrest presented a poem to Henry VIII's son, Edward VI, in which card playing is criticized as tending to idleness, especially when it is pursued by the laboring classes.

Craps might keep them busier.

FAIRS

A Frost Fair was held on the Thames River in London in 1814. It was called that because the winter had been

(CONTINUED) extremely cold,
and huge masses of ice had
come together in the upper
parts of the river early in
January. After that there was
a thaw, and on the thirtieth
the pieces of ice coursed
down the river until the
space between Blackfriars and
and London Bridges became
obstructed.

Then there was a frost,
and the pieces of ice froze
together. On the first of
February there was a
thoroughly solid surface of
ice between Blackfriars and
Three Crane Stairs at the
foot of Queen Street,
Cheapside.

London,
literally
on
ice.

Thousands of Londoners
were attracted to the area
and all kinds of amusements
and activities took place.
One of these was a ceremony

Y'all
come and
bring
your
skates.

UNDER PILLOW WEDDING CAKE
AND OTHER CUSTOMS: ANNOTATED

(CONTINUED)of roasting and toasting a small sheep over a coal fire in a large iron pan. Some enterprising Londoners decided to charge people to watch this curious spectacle and asked the sum of sixpence for a view; the money was paid.

Bleachers or grand-stand?

The delicate meat from the sheep, when done, sold for a shilling a slice and was given the name of "Lapland Mutton."

Terrific name hype. Not just roasted sheep.

Booths were erected all over the place displaying streamers and flags and holiday signs. Beverages and food were also sold, with gin, beer, and gingerbread favorite drinks and goodies.

Better no ice with the gin.

All of this went on the following day and the Thames River was turned literally and practically into a Fair.. and thus the name Frost Fair.

What..no ferris wheels or merry-go-rounds?

(CONTINUED) It was also
called the "City Road" and
all classes of people lined
both sides. Printing presses
were set up and sheets
commemorative of the "Great
Frost",another name for the
event, were published and
eagerly bought.

"Polar Bear" instead of the "Bull-dog" edition.

On the following
Thursday, more people came
to the Fair: swings,dancing,
bookstalls, and other kinds
of amusements took place. On
Friday there were more people
and many pedlars came to sell
their wares at high prices
and making enormous profits.

Pie eating or judging contests? Anything to make a shil-ling or pound.

Books and toys labelled
"Bought on the Thames" were in
great demand. The wind had
shifted to the south, and a
slight fall of snow occurred,
but this didn't dissuade the
continued frenzied multitude

Collect-ibles, too.

(CONTINUED) of people from coming to the fair. The footpath in the center was hard and fairly secure and four donkeys started trotting around the area to every one's amusement.

Maybe "best at fair" in animal judging.

A great deal of gambling was going on and some people lost so much they didn't have a penny left which was needed to cross the plank to get to a dry area on the shore.

Something new, Las Vegas: Blackjack on ice.

Musicians playing violins invited people to dance to merry reels, and folks sat around large fires drinking rum and grog. More conservatice individuals drank tea and coffee. Finally that night the rain began to fall and the temperature started going up: The Frost Fair was no more. The ice was gone, but fun and fond memories remained.

Anything to keep warm.

(CONTINUED)A publication that
had the date of 1641 described
the Bartholomew Fair. Events
and activities of this fair
included drums,hobby-horses,
rattles, babies, pigs and ale.
This fair went on for many
years, and an Almanac for
1677 mentions roast pigs as
being a "greasy feature of
this fair."

The same publication for
1695 mentions farmers at the
fair being instructed as to
what kind of wife they should
choose. The advice given was
to choose a wife that is not
"dressed up in fancy ribbons,
lace, frills, and knots."

The reason? Because such
a wife will be all play and
no work. The farmers were,
thus, in effect, given a
choice as to what kind of
wife they wanted.

Talk
about
diver-
sity.

Eating
or
catching?

Marital
advice
tent
next to
pie
judging
stand.

Farmer:
"I like
that one
with the
'play'
angle."

(CONTINUED)   A   published
Parliamentary Resolution dated
17th July 1651 specifically
directed that an annual fair
at a major city in England not
be held there until
Parliamentary permission is
given.

A rare document dated
1709 gave the reasons for
banning that fair. The
complaint was that the booths
were not for trade, products,
merchandise, or services.

> No hot
> dogs,pies,
> or arts
> and
> crafts.

Instead they were for
drinking, music, gambling,
raffling, shows, stage-plays,
and lotteries.

> The best
> kind of
> fair.

A fair at a certain city
in England on the ninth of
July featured a procession of
men wearing antique armor.
They were preceded by
musicians playing appropriate
music and followed by the

> Walking
> or
> mounted?

UNDER PILLOW WEDDING CAKE
AND OTHER CUSTOMS: ANNOTATED

(CONTINUED) steward of a Manor, peace officers, and well-known inhabitants. This was a traditional ceremony which originated back to a remote period in the history of the place. That was when the town was a highly important and noted wool center.

> Was wool-gathering a popular sport?

Wool merchants and traders came there from all parts of the kingdom. The event was called "Walking the Fair" and typified the armed force necessary to maintain peace and order. That's why they needed men wearing armour.

> Parties must have been really wild and wooly.

An unusual fair didn't take place in a city in England. It was /held on the fourteenth of September and was called the "Fool's Fair." When King William and his Queen were travelling through

> The what?

- 67 -

UNDER PILLOW WEDDING CAKE
AND OTHER CUSTOMS: ANNOTATED

(CONTINUED)the kingdom, they
arrived at this place on
their tour. They asked the
citizens of the town what
they would like, and they,
the people,petitioned his
majesty and said they wanted   Fairs are
a fair.   fun.

It was, however, the
harvest season, and all the
people were working in the
fields. The town had no
industry, no trade, no
manufacturing, and no crafts.

There was no need, no
occasion, no necessity,and
no reason to have a fair;   So what?
there was nothing in that   we can
                                  dream,
community to support that   can't
kind of event. Putting on a   we?
fair was a practical
impossibility.

However,the king smiled
and granted the petition for
a fair. He remarked that

UNDER PILLOW WEDDING CAKE
AND OTHER CUSTOMS: ANNOTATED

(CONTINUED) (the petition)
"was a very humble one,
indeed."

FARMING AND AGRICULTURE

Many years ago, after
farm owners got their harvest
in, they sat down and enjoyed
a lavish feast with their
servants and workers who had
worked for them in the fields.
At this banquet and
entertainment, all were equal
and there was no distinction
between master and servant.

They sat at the same
table together, ate together,
and talked together. There
was dancing and singing for
the rest of the night with
the utmost friendliness among
every one.

The owners were very
grateful and respectful
toward their servants and
workers, realizing that

Hang up
your
sickle
and let's
eat.

They
still
knew
who
was
boss.

Time to
ask
for
a
raise.

(CONTINUED) the harvest was the result of the labors of the workers.

One individual on the farm was usually designated "Lord of the Harvest." This was more than an honorary title; he was described as a sober-working man who was considered an expert regarding all kinds of harvest work.

B.M.O.F.:
Big
Man
on
Field.

He was usually well built and physically strong and often led activities concerning reaping and mowing.

At harvest time various communities had different ceremonies and customs. In certain cities a custom was enjoyed at this season called "Crying the Mare."

Nothing to
do with
horses.

This was done as follows: The reapers tie together the tops of the last blades of

(CONTINUED) corn and that
object is called a "Mare."
Then, standing at some
distance, they throw their
sickles at it; the person who
cuts the knot wins a prize
with lots of cheering and
acclamations.

Onlookers kept their distance.

At another community at
this time, the farmers drove
furiously home with their
last loads of corn on their
carts; when the people saw
this, they ran after the
speeding carts with bowls
full of water.

They threw the water at
the cart, the farmer, and the
corn and at the same time did
a great deal of yelling and
shouting.

No wonder the farmers "drove furiously"

In a Scottish publication
dated 1797 a harvest custom
called a "Maiden Feast" was
described. This event was

UNDER PILLOW WEDDING CAKE
AND OTHER CUSTOMS: ANNOTATED

(CONTINUED) celebrated upon the
finishing of the harvest, and
to prepare for it, the last
handful of corn reaped in the
field was called "The Maiden."
This was generally contrived   Sounds
to fall into the hands of one   like
                                     a
of the beautiful girls in the   set-up.
field.

　　Then that handful of corn
was lovingly dressed up with   The
ribbons and brought home in   girl
                                     too?
triumph with the music of
bagpipes and violins. After
that a fine dinner was given
to every one and the evening
was spent in merrymaking an
dancing.

　　The fortunate girl who
took "The Maiden" was named
the "Queen of the Feast."   Naturally.
This custom later was
abandoned and afterwards each   Bring back
worker was given some money   the
                                     girls.
and a loaf of bread.

- 72 -

UNDER PILLOW WEDDING CAKE
AND OTHER CUSTOMS: ANNOTATED

(CONTINUED)A traveler who was
touring in the Hebrides
reported that he saw a
harvest in a small field in
one of the western islands.
All the workers were singing
a harvest song, and the
singing was timed with the
strokes of the sickles.

Like
rowers
on
ancient
ships.

Songs were sung at other
places during the harvest;
some didn't have much meaning
but they provided regularity
and cheerfulness during the
work.

Who cares,
as long as
the work
was done.

On the island of Minorca
harvests are usually gathered
by the middle of June. As the
corn ripens, many boys and
girls station themselves on
the edges of fields and on
the tops of fence-walls. They
do that to frighten away the
small birds by shouting,
yelling, screaming, and

Juvenile
scare-
crows.

UNDER PILLOW WEDDING CAKE
AND OTHER CUSTOMS: ANNOTATED

(CONTINUED)making a lot of
noise.

One family in Scotland
kept a piper to play to his
workers in the field during
harvest, and, of course paid
him to do this. If any worker
was going too slow, the Piper
was behind him using the
bagpipes to urge him to go
a little faster.

Highland inspiration while they work.

A spritely "Corn or Wheat Symphony"

In the North of England
after the wheat was all cut,
people observed the old
custom of "Crying the Neck."
While the workers were
working on the last field,
one of them most familiar
with the customs of the
season would go around to the
shocks and sheaves and select
a little bundle of the best
he could find.

How's that again?

The best?
Is there a difference in wheat?

This bundle which was
neatly tied up was called

(CONTINUED)"The Neck." After
all the work was done every
one stood round in a circle
in the center of which was the
person with "The Neck." That   The
individual grasped it with   Star.
both hands, stooped down and
held it near the ground.

Meanwhile, all the men
around took off their hats,
stooped down, and held their
hats with both hands
downwards. Every one then
starts yelling and singing   Easy
"The Neck!"...."The Neck!"   words
                                   to
.."The Neck!".."The Neck!."   remember.

While they are singing
and yelling, they raise   Must
themselves upright, and   be
                                   seen
elevate their arms and hats   to be
above their heads.The holder   believed.
of "The Neck" then raises it
on high, and the whole
procedure is repeated three
times, after which they all

(CONTINUED)change their cries
to "wee yen" and "way yen."
The same movements with the
body and arms are done again.
After that every one starts
to laugh in a joyous way and
hats and caps are thrown up
the air.

Get your
own hat or
cap back.

    Next one of the men
takes "The Neck" and runs
very fast to the farmhouse
where one of the young female
houseworkers stands at the
door with a full pail of water
in her hands.

Very fast
if the
girl is
pretty.

    If that man holding "The
Neck" is able to get into the
house by some other means than
the door at which the girl
stands, he could lawfully kiss
her. If he fails, the girl can
dump the pail of water over
him. There was an explanation
for this "Crying the Neck"
ceremony: It was designed to

Can he
then
unlawfully
kiss her?

(CONTINUED)give the surrounding area notice of the end of the harvest."Wee yen" and "Way en" was the rustic way of saying "We end." "The Neck" generally was suspended in the farmhouse sometimes for three or four years.

Why not just ring a bell or blow a horn?

For kissing purposes?

THE FEAST OF SHEEP-SHEARING

On the day they begin to shear their sheep, sheep owners in the South of England provided a lavish and plentiful dinner and feast for the shearers and their friends.

Hopefully they also fed the sheep.

A table was also spread in the open village for the young people and children.The washing and shearing of sheep was considered of great importance and it was a time of fun and festivity.

UNDER PILLOW WEDDING CAKE
AND OTHER CUSTOMS: ANNOTATED

(CONTINUED) The favorite food at the feast was cheese cake. These festivities and celebrations did cost a great deal of money and there were frequent complaints that they were too expensive. One individual complained and said the wages of three shepherds was spent on fresh cheese cakes, spices, and saffron pottage.

Not mutton or lamb chops?

He felt that he got clipped.

THE MOON

The moon has always been of importance with regard to many beliefs and customs. Various ancient publications gave the following advice regarding the phases of the moon: Shear sheep at the increase; chop wood from the full to the change; and gather fruit at the waning.

Any advice to lovers?

If a commoner has a

(CONTINUED) chance to be introduced to a king, he, the commoner, should wait until the moon is in conjunction with the sun when the association of an inferior with a superior is good and productive of profit.

How long a wait?

The moon at that time was also used to forecast the weather. A hazy circle around the moon, it was said, meant rain will come. If the circle was wide and far from the moon, it meant that rain will be delayed for some time.

TV fore-casters take note.

Didn't even use Doppler.

If the circle was close and near the disc, rain will come very soon.

Astrology was also brought into the picture. One piece of advice given was to "purge" the head by sneezing when the moon is in Cancer, Leo, or Virgo.

A lot of fingers under noses while waiting.

UNDER PILLOW WEDDING CAKE
AND OTHER CUSTOMS: ANNOTATED

(CONTINUED) Bathing was advised when the moon was in Cancer, Libra, Aquarius, or Pisces. Cutting the hair or beard was supposed to be done when the moon was in Libra, Sagittarius, Aquarius, or Pisces. When the moon was in Taurus, Virgo, or Capricorn, the time was good for farming and agriculture such as setting, sowing, grafting, and planting.

Barbers as well as lovers gazed at the moon.

The production of corn was favored when the moon was in Cancer, and grafting operations were especially advised to be done in March at the moon's increase, when she is in either Taurus or Capricorn.

Zodiac booklets were probably sold by farm equipment dealers.

There was a prevalent custom in Scotland, particularly in the Highlands where women would curtsy to the new moon and sing a song

Nice gesture.

UNDER PILLOW WEDDING CAKE
AND OTHER CUSTOMS: ANNOTATED

(CONTINUED) asking the moon who her husband will be.After that they would go to bed right away and dream to reveal who their future mates will be. An individual said that he knew two women who did this when they were young maids and they had dreams about the actual men who eventually married them.

Lunar match-maker.

Dream husbands.

ROYAL OAK DAY

Many years ago in the North of England it was the custom for people to wear oak leaves in their hats, and the leaves sometimes had gold-leaf on them. This took place every May twenty-ninth which was the anniversary of the restoration of Charles II. This was done to commemorate the escape of that monarch from his pursuers

A precious fashion.

1660.

(CONTINUED)who actually passed
under the famous oak tree,
later called the Royal Oak,
where he was hiding after the
Battle of Worcester.

The Chase Scene.

The tree was described
as a "bow-shoot" distance
from a house called Boscobel.
It was also near a horse track
passing through the wood. The
king and his companion used a
ladder to climb the tree when
they realized it was no longer
safe to stay in the house.

A royal tree house.

The people in the house
reached to feed them by using
a hook. The Royal Oak tree was
later enclosed with a brick
wall, the inside of which
became covered with laurel.
Close by its side a young
thriving plant grew from one
of its acorns.

A natural honor.

At one city in England
it was customary on September

(CONTINUED)twenty-ninth for
a number of young men dressed
in the style of the
seventeenth century to parade
down the streets. They were
armed with swords and they
gathered contributions from
the spectators.

You <u>do</u> want to contribute don't you?

A man was at the head
and leading   the procession
and he was dressed in black.
His face and hands were
smeared with soot and grease
and his body was bound with
a strong cord; the end of the
cord was held so that the
man could not run too far.

Latest fashion?

After that came another
group, each man dressed like
the man leading the
procession and carrying a
large branch of an oak tree.
Four other men brought up the
rear, carrying a throne made
of oaken boughs. A child sat

Emphasis on oak.

(CONTINUED)on that throne.
Spectators who watched the
parade laughed and amused
themselves by throwing dirt
and stones at the man in black

Real
funzies.

at the head of the procession.
In the evening every one
including spectators and
paraders enjoyed a great

All is
forgiven.

feast which was paid for by
the money that was collected
during the parade.

The swords
came
in handy.

WATER CUSTOM

An ancient event in the
North of England concerned
boys and girls of adjoining
villages meeting as a group
at springs or rivers on a
certain Sunday in May.

They met and enjoyed
themselves by drinking sugar
and water, a treat provided
by the girls. This day was
called "Sugar and Water"

No I.D.s
necessary.

UNDER PILLOW WEDDING CAKE
AND OTHER CUSTOMS: ANNOTATED

(CONTINUED) Sunday. After
that sweet party they all
went to a public house and   Enough
the boys treated this time   sugar
                                    and
with somewhat more   water.
"substantial" goodies
including cakes, ale, and   I.D.S
                                    necessary.
punch.

MUMMING (MASKERS)

        Mumming was a favorite
ceremony and rite during the   There is
                                    now a
holiday and festive season.   New Years
Mummers,who were individuals   Day
                                    Mummers
wearing masks, costumes, and   Parade
disguises,went from house to   in the
                                    U. S.
house spreading holiday cheer
and having a good time with
every one they met.

        There was a great deal
of feasting and presents were
mutually sent;there was also
exchanges of dress and   Grab bags
                                    maybe?
costumes.

        A spectacular Mummery

- 85 -

(CONTINUED) was made by the
citizens of London in 1377
for the entertainment of the
young Prince Richard, the son
of the Black Prince. On a
certain Sunday night, one
hundred and thirty disguised
Mummers on horses rode to
Kennington beside Lambeth
where the young prince stayed
with his mother.

A royal
over- or
under-
whelming.

The Mummers were
accompanied by the music of
cornets and trumpets and the
singing of minstrels. They
also carried torch-lights of
wax.

Forty-eight riders were
in the first rank dressed in
gowns, sandals, and wearing
visors on their faces. After
them came forty-eight knights
dressed the same as the
former group.

Visors for
security
reasons?

Following them was a

- 86 -

(CONTINUED) Mummer dressed
like an emperor, and the rest
of them dressed in costumes
and disguises. Eight or ten
of them had black visors on
their faces. The entire group
entered the Manor of
Kennington, got off their
horses, and entered the hall
on foot.

Privacy reasons.

The Prince, his Mother,
and other people from their
court came out of a chamber
into the hall; they were then
saluted by the Mummers. The
Mummers displayed a pair of
dice and put them on a table.

Royal greetings.

This indicated their
desire to play dice with the
Prince. They played dice, and
the game was arranged so that
the Prince always won.There
were three prizes for him: A
Golden Bowl, a Golden Cup,
and a Golden Ring.

Fourteenth century seven come eleven.

Loaded dice? Even in those days?

(CONTINUED) Then the Mummers
turned to the Prince's Mother,
the Duke, the Earls, and the
other lords for some more   Fixed
                                   game for
gaming, and they all won   them too?
golden rings.

    After the games there was
a grand feast for every one   Lots of
                                   food and
with music; the Prince and the   drinks;
lords danced with the Mummers,   precursor
                                   of
and the Mummers danced with   casinos.
each other. Later they all had
drinks and the Mummers
departed in the same order as
the way they came.

CHRISTMAS CUSTOMS

    On Christmas Eve in
ancient times the people would
light up candles and put a log
of wood on the fire called a
Yule-Clog or Christmas block.
This would make the house warm
and bright.

    In farm houses in the
North of England, the servants

(CONTINUED) would put up a
large knotty block of wood
for their Christmas fire.
During the time it lasted,   Make
                                it
they were entitled, by   a real
custom,to ale at their meals.   big one.

A magazine for February,
1795 published an account of
an interesting custom that
took place on the twenty-   Christmas
                                Eve
fourth of December in   game.
England.

At a house near
Birmingham as soon as supper
was over a table was set in
the hall. A brown loaf of
bread with twenty silver
threepence coins stuck on top   Bread
                                money.
of it; a tankard of ale; and
pipes and tobacco were all
put on the table.

Two chairs were put
behind the table and the two
oldest servants sat there as   All legal
                                like.
"judges."

UNDER PILLOW WEDDING CAKE
AND OTHER CUSTOMS: ANNOTATED

(CONTINUED) An individual
known as the steward brought
the servants in, both men and
women, one at a time. They
were completely covered,with
a sheet for each servant.

No
identity
theft
here.

The right hand of the
servant, and only the right
hand,was put on the loaf of
bread. No other part of the
person's body was exposed.

Not
very
sanitary.

The oldest of the two "judges"
tried to guess who the servant
was by looking at the hand
and saying a name.

No
peeking.

The younger "judge" would
do the same: look at the hand
and mention a name. Then the
older "judge" would go through
the same procedure again. If
both the "judges" guessed the
right name each time, the
steward led the servant away.

No
prints
or DNA
at that
time.

You lost.

If the "judges" don't
guess the right name during

(CONTINUED) the procedure,
the sheet is taken off of the
servant and he or she
receives a threepence coin.
That servant then makes a low
bow to the "judges", doesn't
say a word, and leaves.

Thinking:
"I fooled
you."

Take the
money and
go.

When the next servant
was brought in, the "judges"
switched their guessing: the
younger one guessed first and
third. The procedures were
continued alternatively until
all the money was gone.

Better
accuracy?

Whatever servant had not
slept in the house on the
preceding night forfeited his
or her right to any money.
When the money was all gone,
the servants had full liberty
to drink, dance, sing, and go
to bed whenever they pleased.

There was
always
a
catch.

The
"judges"
too?

CHRISTMAS PIES

Pies made of these
ingredients were very popular

UNDER PILLOW WEDDING CAKE
AND OTHER CUSTOMS: ANNOTATED

(CONTINUED) during the Christmas holidays in England: Chickens, eggs, sugar, raisins, lemon, orange peel, and various spices.

And anything else within reach of the cook.

A pie baked for Henry Grey, Bart, consisted of th following ingredients: Two bushels of flour; twenty pounds of butter; four geese; two turkeys; two rabbits, four wild ducks, two woodcocks; six snipes; four partridges: two curlews; and six pigeons.

What, no beef?

Shovels instead of knives, forks, and spoons.

This pie was close to nine feet in circumference and weighed about twelve stone. It was on a case, with wheels on four legs so it could be rolled to each guest who wanted to partake of it.

Mobile meals.

THE LORD OF MISRULE

In the record of a Christmas celebration in the hall of a certain building

UNDER PILLOW WEDDING CAKE
AND OTHER CUSTOMS: ANNOTATED

(CONTINUED) in 1635 the mock
monarch known as the Lord of
Misrule was described. The
record concerned the
jurisdiction and privileges
of that individual.

He can
dream,
can't
he?

Although he was indeed
a mock monarch, he was treated
with the wonderful luxury and
ceremony as befits a true and
genuine great king. He was
attended by a lord keeper; a
lord treasurer; eight white
staves; the captain of his
band of pensioners; and his
guard.

Read
that,
phony.

What
kind of
staves..
wood or
music?

He dined both in the hall
and in his privy chamber. The
pole-axes for his gentlemen
pensioners were borrowed from
a lord and another lord
supplied him with venison on
demand.

A battle
axe with
long
handle.

The Lord Mayor and
Sheriffs of London gave him

UNDER PILLOW WEDDING CAKE
AND OTHER CUSTOMS: ANNOTATED

(CONTINUED) wine. Like other kings, he received many petitions which he gave to his Master of Requests; he also "knighted" man of his favorite petitioners. His expenses, which came out of his own purse, amounted to two thousand pounds.

Every one wants something, even from a "mock" king.

Cheap for that "royal" experience.

After he was "deposed" the King (the real one) "knighted" him at Whitehall. George Ferrers of Lincoln's Inn was Lord of Misrule for twelve days with King Edward VI when he, King Edward VI, kept his Christmas with open house at Greenwich in 1553. His Majesty was delighted with the diversion.

Phony, too.

"Almost like me."

A Thomas Tooker was elected Lord of Misrule. He decided that he needed a few more titles and assumed the following appellations:

- 94 -

UNDER PILLOW WEDDING CAKE
AND OTHER CUSTOMS: ANNOTATED

(CONTINUED) The most
magnificent and renowned
Thomas; by the favor of
fortune; Prince of Alba
Fortunata; Lord of St.
John's; High Regent of the
Hall; Duke of St. Giles's
Marquis of Magdalen's; and
Landgrave of the Grove.

No mono-grammed shirts or hankies for you.

    Also: Count Palatine of
the Cloysters; Chief Bailiff
of Beaumont; High Ruler of
Rome (Rome was the name of
a piece of land, so called,
near to the end of the walk,
on the north side of Oxon in
England); Master of the Manor
of Walton; Governor of
Gloucester Green; sole
Commander of all Titles,
tournaments, and Triumphs;
and Superintendent in all
Solemnities.

    On Christmas Day in the
morning at daybreak an

UNDER PILLOW WEDDING CAKE
AND OTHER CUSTOMS: ANNOTATED

(CONTINUED) English gentlemen invited all his tenants and neighbors to his hall. Every one feasted with strong beer, toast, sugar, nutmeg, and good Cheshire cheese.

Strong beer at daybreak?

The Hsckin (the great sausage) must be boiled by day-break. If it isn't ready by then, two young men take the maiden (the cook responsible) by the arms and run her around the market-place until she is ashamed of her laziness.

Or else.

That'll teach her.

Every one ate, had a good time, and was welcome which gave rise to the proverb:"Merry in the hall when beards wag all."

Goatees too?

ANCIENT PASTIMES

Governments during ancient times often changed their minds regarding sports

(CONTINUED) and games;
sometimes different ones were
permitted and sometimes they
were suppressed. The people,
however, from various walks
of life, still enjoyed their
recreation and engaged in an
amazing variety of diversions.

Kings,
Queens,
serfs,
and
peasants.

Some of these games and
sports were unusual, to say
the least, and some bizarre.
Many were intriguing,
especially the ones of which
very little information is
known.

How did
they
do
that?

A report of the year
1343 briefly describes some
of these leisure activities.
Very short descriptions are
given, enough to pique a
person's interest. The points;
the goals; the reasons; and
the motives of the following
may not be disclosed. They were
still pastimes that people
played and probably enjoyed.

UNDER PILLOW WEDDING CAKE
AND OTHER CUSTOMS: ANNOTATED

(CONTINUED)* A dance and game
of men and women; the men in
fancy dresses masked, one with
a stag's head, another with
with a bear's head,and a third
with a wolf's head.

Masks
definitely
necessary.

* A tub elevated on a pole,and
three naked boys running at it
with a long stick.

Anything
in
the
tub?

* Playing at dice: one
stakes his cloak against
the others money.

It'll
never
play in
Las Vegas.

* A man leaping through a hoop
held by two men, his clothes
being placed on the other side
for him to leap in.

Medieval
broad
jump.

*Dogs sitting up, and a
man with a stick commanding
them.

Circus
act?

* Boys dressed up as dancing
dogs, passing by a man seated
in a chair with a stick.

How about
some
music?

(CONTINUED) * A man with a
small shield and club
fighting a horse rearing up
to fall on him.

Forget the shield, get out of the way.

* One boy carrying another
with his back upwards, as if
to place him upon a pole and
sort of cushion suspended by
two ropes carried on the
shoulders of two others.

Balancing act.

* Balancing a sword on
on the finger, and a wheel
on the shoulder.

Maybe vaudeville is back.

* A boy seated on a stool
holding up his leg. Another
in a sling made by a rope
round a pulley, holding up
his foot and swung by a
third boy, so that his foot
may come in contact with the
foot of the first boy, who,
if he did not receive the
foot of the swinging boy
properly, would risk a severe
blow on the body.

Must be seen to be believed.

UNDER PILLOW WEDDING CAKE
AND OTHER CUSTOMS: ANNOTATED

(CONTINUED) * A dancing bear with a man holding something not understood in his hand.

Does he know what he's holding? Whip? Weapon?

* Two boys drawing a third with all their force seated on a stool (on which is a saddle) running on four wheels.

Medieval kiddy car.

* A man laid on his belly upon a long stool, his head hanging over a vessel with water at the bottom; another man standing at the other end of the stool to lift it up and plunge the head of the first man in the water.

Any volunteers?

* Two boys carrying a third upon a stick thrust between his legs who holds a chicken in his hands. They are followed by another boy with a flag.

Like hobby-horse but with a chicken.

UNDER PILLOW WEDDING CAKE
AND OTHER CUSTOMS: ANNOTATED

(CONTINUED) * Five women seated, a sixth kneeling and leaping upon her hands. One of them lifts her garments over her head which the rest seem to be buffeting.

Peek-a-boo.

* A boy seated cross-legged upon a pole supported by two stools over a tub of water, in one hand holding something not understood, in the other, apparently a candle.

Nothing like being definite.

* The game of "Frog in the Middle You Cannot Catch Me."

Oh, _that_ game!

* Three boys on stools, in a row striking at each other.

They won't be on stools long.

* Two men seated feet to feet, pulling at a stick with all their might.

Ancient tug-of-stick?

* Two men balancing in their hands a long board on which a boy is kneeling on one knee with three swords,

No one sneeze.

(CONTINUED) forming (by their points meeting) a triangle, and to music.

* A man hanging upon a pole, with his elbows and feet together, and his head between his hams, supported by two other men.

His head between his what?

* Three figures with their hands elevated, as if to clap them together; one of them has his fingers bent, as if taking a pinch of snuff.

We saw you.

* Four men, one putting his hand upon the head of a fifth who sits in the middle cross-legged and cross-armed; the rest seem as if advancing to strike him open-handed.

Not exactly fair play.

Middle man leave now.

* A dance of seven men and seven women holding hands.

Alleman left and do-si-do.

UNDER PILLOW WEDDING CAKE
AND OTHER CUSTOMS: ANNOTATED

BOXING

In ancient times if two
boys in an English town
quarrel in the street and the
quarrel turns into a physical
fight, spectators quickly
make a ring around them.
The two then continue to
fight or box after pulling
off their respective ties and
waistcoats.

No
identi-
fying
colored
trunks.

Some even strip down to
their respective waists. They
start by fiercely brandishing
their fists in the air aiming
at the faces, then by kicking
each others shins and grabbing
hair.

Jabs
are
always
effective

Not
exactly
the
Marquis
of
Queens-
bury
Rules.

If one boy knocks the
other boy down, the one
standing can hit the one on
the ground one or two times
again but no more. If the boy
on the ground keeps getting
up, the one standing is

(CONTINUED) obliged to keep hitting him as often as he requires hitting. During the fight, the spectators encourage both boxers enthusiastically and nobody tries to part them during clinches.

> Until he can't get up?
>
> No neutral corners.
>
> No referees.
>
> No mandatory eight-counts.

These street fights and boxing activities draw large crowds of men from all walks of life and social classes. If the parents of the boys are present they let them fight and cheer for the boy who is getting a lot of punishment and possibly may be losing.

If a coachman (buggy or other horse-drawn vehicle driver) has a dispute about the fare with a gentleman who has hired him, and the gentleman offers to fight him to decide the quarrel the

> Look at the meter, Sir.

(CONTINUED) coachman gladly consents. When this happens, the gentleman pulls off his sword and lays it aside along with his cane, gloves, and tie.

A fair fighter.

If the coachman is thoroughly beaten, and he usually is because a gentleman won't do this unless he is sure he can win, that victory goes for payment of the fare. If the coachman wins, the gentleman must pay the fare amount as specified by the driver.

What's the odds?

How about a tip?

CAT AND DOG

There are three players in this ancient game, and clubs are used. Two holes in the ground are dug, each about a foot in diameter and seven inches in depth. The holes are about twenty-six feet apart. A player stands

Played by humans.

(CONTINUED) at each hole with a club, and these clubs are called Dogs. A piece of wood about four inches long and one inch in diameter called a Cat is thrown from one hole toward the other by the third person.

Predecessor of the hockey stick.

Quite different from a puck.

The object of the sport is to prevent the Cat from getting into a hole by the player standin at that hole. Every time the Cat enters a hole, the player who has the Dog at that hole loses the Dog, and he who threw the Cat gets possession both of the Dog and the hole.

As simple as that.

The former possessor of of the Dog then takes charge of the Cat. If the Cat is hit, the player who hits it changes places with the player who holds the Dog. As often as these positions are

(CONTINUED) changed,
co-winners are declared by
the two who hold both clubs
who are viewed as partners.

The
score-
keeper
just quit.

BUCKLER-PLAY

Buckler-Play was a
description of men called
"gladiators" who were seen
marching through the streets
years ago with their sleeves
rolled up carrying swords.
They were preceded by a
drummer who tried to gather
spectators.

Definitely
the
non-Roman
type.

People paid a certain
amount to see the fight,
which was with cutting
swords and a kind of buckler
for defence. The edge of the
sword was a little blunted,
and the care of the prize-
fighters (as they were
called) was to avoid
wounding each other too

Curbside
and
ringside.

From
"buckle"..
to gird
with a
shield and
sword.

(CONTINUED) seriously. They were, however, expected to put up a good fight with plenty of action and lots of aggressiveness, otherwise the people could not be expected to pay and watch. There is no information as to whether or not formal rounds were announced and timed.

Money back guarantee?

Pretty girls with placards?

This type of fighting became very rare within eight to ten years of the time it started. Fights with cudgels (short, thick sticks) also took place; a small wicker basket covering the handle of the stick also covered the hand as a sort of defensive measure.

Possible revival of this sport?

ARCHERY

Archery was one of the sports that the British Government encouraged during ancient times. During the

(CONTINUED)reign of Henry II
it was very popular among
the youth of London.Statutes
passed from the thirteenth
to the sixteenth centuries
actually enforced the use of
the bow; the law mandated and
directed that holiday
leisure time should be
devoted to its practice.

No video games at that time.

Bullseyes instead of spas.

At the time of the
Hundred Years' War, men
making less than a certain
salary were told that they
had to practice archery when
they had nothing else to do.

Put those playing cards away,pick up the bows.

About the year 1753 an
organization called the
Society of Archers was formed
in the metropolis (probably
London.) Targets were erected
during the Easter and Whitsun
holidays, and the best
shooter was named the Captain
and the next best marksman

(CONTINUED)was called the Lieutenant for the ensuing year. Later on the Society was incorporated in the Archers' Division of the Artillery Company. Archery revived again as a general amusement about 1789 when Societies of Toxophilites were formed almost throughout the kingdom, but the sport soon declined.

Officers of the bow.

Or drafted, maybe.

Arrows in the caissons.

Greek: toxon: bow. philos: fond of.

GOLF

Golf is considered one of the most ancient games played with a ball and also using a club. The club was also called a "bandy" because it was bent, and the game itself many years ago was called "bandy-ball." Goff was another ancient name for the pastime.

Iron or wood?

Golf was fashionable

(CONTINUED) among the nobility in the opening of the seventeenth century, and was one of the exercises with which Prince Henry, eldest son of James I occasionally diverted himself.

Diamond studded golf bags.

According to one story, the Prince was playing golf one day and was being watched by his schoolmaster. He, the Prince warned his teacher to stand clear and away from where he was teeing off.

Why aren't you studying? Concentration is important, too.

The pedagogue, however was busily engaged in talking to some one and came too close. The Prince was about to lift his club and start his swing when some one standing near him exclaimed: "Beware that you not hit Master Newton (the schoolmaster!"

No time or place for a lecture.

A tempting situation for the Prince.

The Prince stopped just

(CONTINUED) in time and said: "If I had hit him I would be in deep trouble!"

No high marks for you.

The ball used at this time was stuffed very hard with feathers. An article in the "Gentleman's Magazine" for February 1795 mentions "shinty match", a game somewhat similar to golf.

Forget long drives.

Shinty Match Country Club. Exclusive? Very.

It was popular in the North of Britain. One authority defines "shinty" as an inferior species of golf generally played by young people. He adds that in London it is called "hockey."

NHL take note.

BARLEY BREAK

This is a game generally played by young people in a corn yard. It was also called "Barla-bracks About the Stacks" in the North of Scotland.

(CONTINUED)One stack is
decided on as the "dule" or
goal and one person is
appointed to catch the rest
of the group who run out from
the "dule."

Also
known as
"it."

How many
are in
there?

No
peeking.

    The appointed person
doesn't leave the area until
all the group are out of his
sight.Then he or she goes off
to catch and find them. Any
one who is caught cannot run
around again and is called a
"prisoner," and must help the
captor in trying to catch the
rest. When all are taken the
game is finished and the
first person taken is the
appointed person in the next
game.

Yearsago
called
"Hide
and Go
Seek."

No
prizes
but
sheer and
wild
excite-
ment.

LOGGATS

    Exactly what Loggats are
is not known, but they are
also defined as bone pins.
A stake was put into the

(CONTINUED)ground and the
players threw bone pins at
it. The player who threw
nearest to the stake won.
The game was seen played in
different countries at
sheep-shearing feasts;the
winner was entitled to a
black fleece. (The coat of
wool covering a sheep or
shorn from it.)

Like
horseshoe
pitching.

A
ringer.

    Afterwards the victor
presented the fleece to the
farmer's maid to be spun into
a petticoat; the girl
received the item on the
condition of her kneeling
down on the fleece to be
kissed by all the rustics
present.

Looks nicer
on her
than on
him.

The
real
winners.

PALL MALL

    According to a
publication called "The
French Garden" dated 1621,
the word "Pall Mall" is

UNDER PILLOW WEDDING CAKE
AND OTHER CUSTOMS: ANNOTATED

(CONTINUED) derived from the
French "paille mail" which
is a wooden hammer affixed
to the end of a long staff.
The hammer was used to
strike a bowl, and this was a
game popular with the nobility
and gentry in France.

Not quite like a golf club.

Was the bowl empty?

A further description
and variation from a French
dictionary states that this
is a game in which a round
ball is struck with a mallet
(a paille mail) through a
high arch of iron.

Aerial croquet.

The winner is the
individual who can accomplish
this with the fewest blows or
within a number previously
agreed upon. The locale of
the game mentioned in "The
French Garden" was an alley
in which there were two
arches, one at either end.
This was a fashionable

Par what?

Proper goals.

UNDER PILLOW WEDDING CAKE
AND OTHER CUSTOMS: ANNOTATED

(CONTINUED) amusement in the
reign of Charles II of France
and when people went for a
walk in the area, the place
was called the Mall. The name
was derived from the
circumstances of its having
been used for the playing of
the game by the monarch and
his courtiers.

Wig
cleaners?

Valet
carriage
parking?

ANCIENT LOVE

According to
authoritative reports
extraordinary medicines were
often advertised on the back
pages of newspapers and
sometimes the medications
included items to stimulate
love.

Primitive
aphrodi-
siacs.

These were used, of
course, by people who wanted
to arouse the love of a
possibly romantically
stubborn friend. A writer
about love in 1602 mentions

- 116 -

(CONTINUED) many methods by
which a lover might try to
convince another of his or
her effections. These
included secret
sleight, cunning, drinks,
drugs, medicines, charmed
potions, passion philters,
devices, practices, figures,
and characters.

Also known
as"lines".
Medieval
boiler-
makers;
Mickey
Finns.

The word "Botanomancy"
was often mentioned which
refers to the noise bay
leaves make when they are
crushed between the fingers.
That method, and the Pagan
way of crushing poppies
between the hands was
considered a potent way of
convincing some one of
serious love intentions.

Audio
passion.

Romance
from the
garden.

A comedy dated 1696
entitled "The Mock Marriage"
gave some advice to lovers
as follows: Hide some

UNDER PILLOW WEDDING CAKE
AND OTHER CUSTOMS: ANNOTATED

(CONTINUED) Dazy-roots under your pillow and hang your shoes out of the window. This was a love charm to cause a person to dream of his or her lover.

Clean the roots first

Hopefully, no shoe swipers around.

FARMING CHARMS

A man named Sir Thomas Browne mentioned a rural charm to prevent dodder, tetter, and strangling weeds. He advises placing a chalked tile at the four corners of the farmer's field, and one in the middle of the field. Browne explains his method by admitting that it sound ridiculous in the intention, but rational in the contrivance or act of planning. The purpose of all this was to diffuse the magic through all parts of the area.

An individual named

The tetter weeds are the worst.

Rubber tile? Terrazzo? Cork? Plastic?

No kidding.

That explains everything.

(CONTINUED) Braithwaite
describes a balladmonger
(probably a troubador) who
goes around the country
singing songs that people
enjoy very much. The songs
become very common and
milk-maids sing and chant
those songs while milking
cows. They think that by
doing this the cow will be
charmed to produce more milk.

Rock or Doo-wop?

Are they trying to pull something?

An ancient charm
concerns a person who likes
to walk a lot. According to
this belief if that individual
puts mugwort (wormwood--in
the thistle family) in his or
her shoes in the morning, he
or she will be able to walk
forty miles before noon and
not be tired.

Joggers take note

Pharmaceutical firms take note.

If the seed of fleabane
(thistle family) is strewed
between bed sheets, it is

UNDER PILLOW WEDDING CAKE
AND OTHER CUSTOMS: ANNOTATED

(CONTINUED)believed that
this will cause chastity.
If a person eats comin
(cumin--a plant of the
parsley family,) and then
breathes on some one wearing
make-up on their face, the
make-up will completely
disappear according to
certain beliefs.

For fleas
or humans?

Good-bye
creams and
lotions.

An interesting charm
involved a strong scented,
weedy old world herb called
tansey. Women were advised
to take wild tansey and soak
it in buttermilk for nine
days.

How
strongly
scented?

After that, if they
washed their faces with that
solution, they would become
very attractive. An ancient
belief was that moonwort
(any fern of the genus
botrychium) would open the
locks of houses if it is put
in the key holes.

Beauty at
what price?
"Strongly
scented?

Lockout
solution or
thief
helper?

- 120 -

UNDER PILLOW WEDDING CAKE
AND OTHER CUSTOMS: ANNOTATED

(CONTINUED) A writer named
Leigh noted in his 1647
publication that laurel was
supposed to have wonderful
powers of protection against
lightning. The Roman emperor
Tiberius was terrified of
both thunder and lightning,
and whenever the weather
looked threatening he always
had a chaplet or wreath of
laurel around his neck.

A natural
rod.

Along
with or
instead
of ties
he got
for
holidays?

Augustus was also
afraid of thunder and
lightning and carried a
seal's skin around with him
as protection. The actual
name of the animal was
"Sea-Calfe."

Seals in
Rome?
Interest-
ing comb-
ination.

A publication called
Hill's "Natural and
Artificial Conclusions"
(1670) provides what could
be called a unique means for
protecting a house from

(CONTINUED) thunder and lightning: plant the herb housleek also called syngreen on top of the house.

New agricultural concept: "Roof Farming"

A letter from a Professor Playfair dated 26th January 1804 tells of rural charms at various places. One of them concerns private breweries: it was a practice at many of them to throw a live coal into the brewing vat to avert bad influences.

Does your beer taste different lately?

Another charm involved cow's milk; it was believed that it was a good idea to pass a burning coal across a cow's back and under her belly immediately after she was milked. The reason was that her milk would supposedly be of top quality if they did this.

Careful.. there might be meat on the table as well as milk. Dairy farmers take note.

People who had a

UNDER PILLOW WEDDING CAKE
AND OTHER CUSTOMS: ANNOTATED

(CONTINUED) problem of cows wandering into their houses were advised to do the following: suspend vessels over the fire by an iron chain hanging from a hook. This chain was adjustable up and down and the cows were said to be stopped by raising the vessels a few links.

Better idea:keep the door closed.

Otherwise: bovine citations.

A person named Martin tells about something he saw or heard about in the Western Islands. By means of a charm or other secret method a woman was able to convey the increase of her neighbor's cows' milk to her, the woman's own use. However, the "swiped" milk didn't produce the ordinary quantity of butter.

What did the cows have to say about this?

Serves her right for stealing.

ONIONS WILL TELL

Young girls in ancient

UNDER PILLOW WEDDING CAKE
AND OTHER CUSTOMS: ANNOTATED

(CONTINUED) times, like
present ones, were curious
as to whom their future
husbands will be. They had
a novel, to say the least,
method of getting this
information. They took four,
five, or eight onions and
gave each onion the name of
a possible future spouse.

Sir Tom,
Sir Dick,
or
Sir Harry?

True
romance.

They then put the onions
near a chimney, left them
there and watched them over
a period of time. As soon as
one of the onions sprouted,
they checked the name, and
he would be their future
husband.

Did the
guys know
about
this?

Another method was
used to find out the
feelings and personality
of a future mate. A group
of girls would go to a stack
of wood during the dark of
night and stand near the

Bring your
own
flashlight.

(CONTINUED) wood pile. Each girl would then pull a stick of wood out of the pile; if that stick was straight and clean with no knots, her husband would be a fine and gentle man. If, on the other hand, the stick was crooked and rough with lots of knots, the man would be crabby and irritable.

Only one stick to a girl, please.

Are second chances allowed?

MUSIC

There were many poet musicians during these time periods who wandered around Europe. In France they were called Jongleurs and Troubadours. Skald was their name in Scandinavian countries, and in Ireland it was Bard.

Keeping up with the "Top 40" wasn't easy.

The poet musicians of England were called minstrels who were professionals and got paid in money or gifts

Flat fees or percentages?

(CONTINUED) for their various entertaining services. Besides traveling, many minstrels were members of the households of kings and nobelmen. When traveling, they entertained at castles along their way and also for village folk.

Steady work; maybe even a contract.

Wide ticket cost range.

Some of them composed their own songs and made up stories; other minstrels repeated folk tales and ballads. By doing this, they helped preserve the contemporary material. Many minstrels also played musical instruments.

Rock and roll madrigals.

"Stand-Up" lore.

Using those instruments, they were often utilized for another useful and important duty: they acted somewhat like guards in towers at city and village gates. If they saw an impending attack by enemy forces they would play their

Civic security.

(CONTINUED)instruments as loudly as possible in order to call out the soldiers to prepare defenses.

Sound the alarm in major keys.

ALL FOOLS' DAY/APRIL FOOLS DAY

A publication dated 1760 described one of the ancient pranks that were pulled on people on April Fools Day. Individuals would be sent on what was termed "sleeveless errands." The errands were to get ridiculous and non-existent items and make fools of the people trying to find the things.

We now call them wild goose chases.

Like maybe elbow grease.

A belief concerning April Fools Day was in regard to strange, weird, uncanny, and odd effects the day supposedly and reputedly had on people.

It was said that it was easy to lie to some one on

(CONTINUED) that day. Money lenders would lend money on bad security. Experienced women would marry very disappointing young men. Mathematicians found themselves making mistakes in their figuring.

Sub-primes in those days too?

No D & B s then.

No calculators.

Alchemists were going wrong in their pursuit of the Philosopher's Stone. Politicians were going wrong with regard to their judgement.

Like, forget it already.

So what else is new?

A British publication of 1708 discussed the possible beginning of the April Fools Day customs. One conjecture was that the custom started in the time of the Romans who wanted Sabine wives. (The Sabines were an ancient tribe of Italy who became merged with the Romans.)

UNDER PILLOW WEDDING CAKE
AND OTHER CUSTOMS: ANNOTATED

(CONTINUED) The Romans tried
to get the women by peaceful
means, but they were
unsuccessful, so they, the
Romans, decided on some
strategy. Games in honor of
Neptune were instituted and
performed at the beginning of
April according to the Roman
calendar. Rome was the site.

Romantic
persuas-
ion
didn't
work.

Read that
trickery.

The games were very
exciting and included
wonderful celebrations.
Word got around fast about
all the fun and excitement,
and people flocked to Rome
to join in the festivities.
The Sabines also joined, and
the Romans moved in and
grabbed the women.

Y'all
come.
(Sabines
too)

Didn't
the
Sabines
suspect
something?

April Fool
romance.

ALE

According to ancient
authorities investigating
the etymology of the word
"ale," the major opinion

(CONTINUED) seemed to be that it simply meant "feast," "merry-making," "party," or even "banquet." The word "ale" was added to other words concerning a wide variety of individuals, animals, locations, seasons, etc., etc.

Maybe cart-gate, coach-gate, or even tail-gate parties.

These included "Leet-Ale," "Lamb-Ale," "Whitson-Ale," "Clerk-Ale," "Bride-Ale," "Church-Ale," "Scot-Ale," and "Midsummer-Ale."

Call it anything, just keep the mugs filled.

Ale was the major drink at all these feasts, and from the standpoint of metonymy (a figure of speech in which the name of one thing is put for another associated with it,) "ale" and "feast" came together.

A natural combination.

SWORD DANCE

Historically speaking,

UNDER PILLOW WEDDING CAKE
AND OTHER CUSTOMS: ANNOTATED

(CONTINUED) sword dances were
known during the fourteenth,
fifteenth, and sixteenth
centuries. A history book
concerning the "Northern
Nations" reports that the
Northern Goths and Swedes
had a sport consisting of a
dance with swords that was
performed in a certain formal
manner.

Before
or after
the
smorgas-
bord?

First the dancers would
dance in a triple round with
their swords sheathed and
erect in their hands; then
they would draw their swords
and again hold them erect as
before.

Don't
get too
close.

After that they would
extend them (the swords)
from hand to hand and lay
hold of each others hilts
and points. "Hilts and
Points" meant that a dancer
would hold a hilt (the
handle) of a sword in his

Ticklish,
but no
laughing.

- 131 -

UNDER PILLOW WEDDING CAKE
AND OTHER CUSTOMS: ANNOTATED

(CONTINUED) right hand and
the point of the next
performer's sword in his left
hand. While they were doing
this, they would change their
dancing order and form
themselves into a figure of
a hexagon which they called a
rose.

No arabes-
ques or
pirouettes
allowed.

After that movement,
they would raise and draw
back their swords undoing the
hexagon and forming a
four-square rose. As a finale
they dance rapidly backwards
rattling the sides of their
swords together. There were
often pipes or songs
accompanying the dance which
often started slow, but
increased in speed afterwards
to the conclusion.

A choreo-
grapher's
challenge
or
nightmare.

Terpsicho-
rean
defiance.

WEATHER OMENS

Forecasting and
predicting the weather was

- 132 -

UNDER PILLOW WEDDING CAKE
AND OTHER CUSTOMS: ANNOTATED

(CONTINUED) quite popular in
ancient times, and the human
body was often used for this
purpose. Bodily aches and
pains and corns on the feet
were supposed to be a means
to portend the climate.

Rheumat-
ism in
those
days?

Those problems were
supposed to mean either rain
or frost. Furthermore, aches
were said to make the humours
(Vital fluids of the body
according to ancient
physicians) active. Corns on
the feet were said to make
the humours sharper.

Quite
a
range.

Not too
sharp.

Animals were also
involved in climatological
matters. If the tail of a
heifer (a young cow that has
not had a calf) was sticking
straight up, rain was
expected.

Televis-
ion
forcast-
ers take
note.

A publication in 1664
called "The Husbandman's

(CONTINUED) Practice" wrote about other signs of rain including ducks and drakes shaking and fluttering their wings when they rise from the water,and young horses rubbing their backs against the ground.

Maybe only for aerodynamic reasons.

Rain and itching reasons.

Rain was also indicated when sheep were seen bleating, playing, or skipping wantonly. Other approaching rain signs included swine being seen to carry bottles of hay or straw to any place and hide them; oxen licking themselves against the hair; the sparkling of a lamp or candle; frogs croaking; and swallows flying low.

Also practicing to help sleepers.

Piggy express, but can they find them later?

Fleas maybe?

Considering pigs and hogs, a publication called the "Cabinet of Nature" (1637) states that when a

UNDER PILLOW WEDDING CAKE
AND OTHER CUSTOMS: ANNOTATED

(CONTINUED group of hogs run crying home, this is a sign of an impending rain storm. That same publication gives the reason for this belief: the hog is a very dull animal and of a melancholy nature.

Either that or they are homesick.

A weather predictor and not that dull.

Staying on the farm, cattle and donkeys will supposedly prick up their respective ears foretelling rain. Another omen: when the down flies off of colts-foot, dandelion, and thistles and there is no wind, it is an indication of rain.

Meteorolgists take note.

AMUSING TRENCH

Country homes in certain areas of the world had a ditch constructed around the building to keep animals and invaders out.It was called a HaHa and was built below the level of the ground usually

Bill collectors too, maybe.

Ancient booby trap.

UNDER PILLOW WEDDING CAKE
AND OTHER CUSTOMS: ANNOTATED

(CONTINUED) with one side
sloping and the other side
steep. Sometimes, however,
both sides were built sloping.   Trapping
A wall was built along the   efficiency.
bottom.

    It probably got the
name HaHa from individuals
who inadvertently stepped or   Droll
fell into it or possibly when   humor.
some one saw a friend or enemy
fall into it. The humor of the   Real
                                     funzies!
situation may not always have
been appreciated, but the name
obviously seemed very apt.

PRESENTS FOR A GENTLEMAN'S GENTLEMAN
    The word "livery" often
brings to mind in many people
the colors worn by jockeys in   Especially
                                     the
a horse race. This is, of   winner.
course, true but going bac
many years there was a wider
aspect to its meaning.
    It originally concerned   New or
                                     used
the clothes a man gave to his   clothes?

UNDER PILLOW WEDDING CAKE
AND OTHER CUSTOMS: ANNOTATED

(CONTINUED) butler and it also was in regard to the stable where the horses were kept. Other members of a royal household such as cooks, maids, footmen, gardeners, etc., etc. were also often given beautiful clothes and uniforms.

Was the butler kept there, too?

"We like fashions too!"

The same was true of lords and barons and their respective households. A further extension of the word "livery" was the phrase "Livery Companies." This was about members of certain groups who belonged to a medieval trade or guild; the members wore special clothing (livery) to identify their respective organizations.

Not to be outdone by the king.

Butcher, Baker, Candle-stick Maker.

FUN WITH SAILORS

Sailors used to engage in many sports on the high seas. One trick involved a

Like swabbing the deck?

(CONTINUED) non-sailor (probably a passenger) while sailing in the warm latitudes. A large tub was filled with water and two stools were placed on either side of the tub.

Included in the fare cost.

Passenger: "Looks interesting."

An old sail or tarpaulin was placed over all this; the cloth was held there very tightly by two individuals who sat on the stools on either side of the tub.

Passenger: "Looks like a fun game!"

The two persons on the stools represented the King and Queen of a foreign country. The individual who had the dubious "honor" of participating was called the "Ambassador."

Marine Royalty

He then had to repeat a stupid and ridiculous speech which was dictated to him after which he was solemnly conducted up to the "Throne."

Part of the solemn ritual.

(CONTINUED) The throne was, of course, in the middle of the cloth stretched between the two stools. Again, with the greatest solemnity, he was invited to sit on the "Throne;" as soon as the poor individual sat down the Royal Functionaries on either side stood up and the "Ambassador" got a dunking.

Where else?

Passenger: "I'm getting suspicious!"

"KING ARTHUR"

This was another sport among sailors. A sailor called "King Arthur" would sit near a large tub of water and he would be dressed in a ridiculous outfit. He wore a wig made of oakum and old rags.

Fun on the high seas.

Not exactly royal clothes.

Another member of the crew, after being formally introduced, was required to pour a bucket of water over him with the polite greeting

Congratulations, coach! Your team won!

(CONTINUED)"Hail King Arthur"
The sailor doing the pouring
was forbidden to laugh or
smile while dumping the
water;the man sitting down
and getting drenched,however,
played the clown and made
funny faces and motions.If
the sailor doing the pouring
even cracked a smile, he
would have to become "King
Arthur" and get the dunking.

Absolutely
poker
face.

Medieval
sit-down
comedian.

A PRIZE OF BACON

At Essex in England
anciently there was an annual
custom of giving a piece of
bacon to the married couple
who would swear to a serious
oath.

Both had
to do
this.

They had to swear that
neither of them, in a year
and a day, either sleeping or
waking,had repented of their
marriage. The couple were
required to take this oath

Even if
the husband
snored?

Or the
wife
couldn't
cook?

(CONTINUED) before every
one in town. According to
the inscription on a print
showing the ceremony, after
delivery of the bacon the
happy pair were transported
around on men's shoulders in
a chair reserved for that
occasion.

Still on
that
little
pink
cloud.

They were carried
around to the accompaniment
of minstrels, drums, and
other music; the piece of
bacon was borne on a high
pole in front of them.

Couple:
"We're
getting
hungry"

The procession was
attended by the steward,
gentlemen, and officers of
the manor plus inferior
tenants carrying wands and
other emblems of office.

What
about the
superior
tenants?

The crowd grew bigger
with a group of bachelors
and maidens, six of each sex
walking two and two plus a

(CONTINUED)vast multitude of people from adjacent towns and villages. Parades and celebrations marked this occasion. The couple in the chair were the center of attraction for hundreds of merrymaking people.

Couple to each other: Maybe we should have repented."

CARNIVAL TIME

Many years ago, Carnival Time was a real fun occasion when people engaged in somewhat unusual, to say the least, pastimes. When a lady spotted a man that she knew and liked or didn't know but still thought she might like, she threw oranges at him.

Anything, but anything goes.

No ERAs at that time.

If the guy got hit in the eye with an orange it meant only one thing: the girl who threw the orange liked him very much and maybe even loved him.

"I didn't know you cared"

(CONTINUED) If a man got hit in his mouth with one of the oranges and a tooth was knocked out, he was definitely the object of that female orange-throwers affection.

A simple love note would do.

Who paid the Dentist's bill?

FOOL PLOUGH

This ceremony was also called Plough Monday, and reports during the years of 1493, 1494, 1522, 1542, and 1575 mention this custom and rite.

Long span; fifteenth and sixteenth centuries.

The procedure was actually called Fool Plough in the North of England, and the pageant consisted of a number of sword dancers dragging a plough with music.

Did a person have to be one? (A Fool.)

Were the horses on strike?

One and sometimes two of the draggers were dressed in strange clothing and had interesting names: one was

(CONTINUED) called Bessy in the attire of a woman and the other was called the Fool. He, the Fool, was almost completely covered with animal skins and wore a hairy cap. The tale from some animal hung from his back.

Talk about an apt name.

The official duty of one of these involved characters was to go among the spectators displaying and rattling a box asking for donations.

No free entertain- ment and no free Fools.

Another name for this rite was the White Plough because the gallant young men pulling the ploughs were dressed in their white shirts and not wearing coats or waistcoats.

Laundry business shares went up.

Ribbons folded into roses were stitched on the shirts. The season was actually cold, so the boys

The latest plough-pull fashions.

- 144 -

(CONTINUED)(secretly) wore
warm waistcoats under their
shirts. They drew the plough
all around the town and if
some houses didn't
appreciate these activities
the draggers would draw the
plow in front of the houses
forming furrows (trenches
made by ploughs.) One
report said that twenty men
were pulling one plough.

The exact meaning for
all these activities is
obscure, but there have been
theories that call them a
rural triumph or victory.
The victory over who, what,
why, and where was not
disclosed.

An English publication
dated 1710 was asked about
Plough Monday and they
answered that it was a
country phrase only used by

No
peeking.

You
would
rather
have a
farm than
a lawn
wouldn't
you?

Give the
horses a
contract.

One dragger
to the
other:"Why
are we
doing
this?"

We got a
winner, so
who cares?

UNDER PILLOW WEDDING CAKE
AND OTHER CUSTOMS: ANNOTATED

(CONTINUED) peasants. They would get together at that time and meet over a cup of ale and some good food. They would wish each other a plentiful harvest and salute the plough when they started to break ground.

Any excuse or no excuse for a party.

Horses this time.

Another Plough Monday activity involved a friendly contest between the men and the women. In the morning they would strive to see who could get up the earliest.

Roosters but no clock radios.

If the men could get their whip, staff, hatchet, and other tools by the fireside before the women got the kettles of food cooking, the men won. After all this contesting they would all have a good supper and some strong drink. This is the way young people were attracted to farming.

Confusion in the kitchen.

Main attraction: food and strong drink.

- 146 -

UNDER PILLOW WEDDING CAKE
AND OTHER CUSTOMS: ANNOTATED

UNBELIEVABLE BELIEFS

Folklore is loaded with anecdotes, tales, stories and especially beliefs involving an assortment of humans, animals, birds, and objects.

Fascinating area.

During the sixteenth, seventeenth, and eighteenth centuries people believed things that ranged from the astounding to the ridiculous to the amazing. Many of the beliefs were far-fetched and ludicrously unlikely.

All quite amusing though.

Some people thought all of them were true, some thought much of them were true, others questioned the validity of the beliefs, and others flatly denied them.

Degrees of gullibility.

The following is presented on the basis of so-called "authoritative" publications and writers of the aforementioned time periods.

UNDER PILLOW WEDDING CAKE
AND OTHER CUSTOMS: ANNOTATED

BARNACLES

Barnacles as every one knows are a kind of shellfish that attaches itself to the bottoms of rocks, ship bottoms, wharf piles, turtles, and whales. They belong to the subclass Cirripedia, and they also stick to floating pieces of wood.

Man the scrapers, boys.

It was thought many years ago that when a barnacle broke off the bottom of a ship or whatever it was attached to, it became a species of goose.

A gentleman named Holinshed declared that with his own eyes he saw feathers at least two inches long hanging out of the shell of a barnacle.

Time to change that whiskey brand.

A writer named Gerard declared that in the northern parts of Scotland there are

(CONTINUED)certain trees
that grow shellfishes, and
when these shellfishes fall
into the water they become
fowls, which we call
barnacles. These "fowls"
were called "Brant Geese"
in the north of England and
in Lancanshire,"Tree Geese."

Talk about searches for identity.

There is also a species
of wild goose called the
"Brent Goose" found in
Germany, which is also
called the "duck-mussel."

More confusion.

Scientifically speaking
there are presently three
types of recognized
barnacles: the acorn
barnacle; the common rock
barnacle; and the goose
barnacle.

Here we go again.

DARK LANTERNS

Years ago a writer named
Barrington wrote about
curfews in his "Observations

(CONTINUED)on the Ancient
Statutes."In this publication
he said there is a belief to
the effect that is is illegal
and unlawful to go about with
a dark lantern.

Any one
got
a light?

He also stated that all
popular errors have some
foundation and the curfew may
have something to do with
the dark lantern law. A dark
lantern means, of course an
unlit lantern, and the
relationship between that and
the curfew may only be known
by Barrington.

Black laws
rather than
blue laws.

Candle
black
market?

One reason may be that
if any one is out at night
after curfew they should walk
around with an unlit lantern
so as not to be apprehended
or arrested.

Lost maybe,
but at
least
not
picked
up.

OSTRICHES

There was a widespread
belief that ostriches eat and

(CONTINUED)digest iron. A
writer named Ross quotes a
Doctor Brown who flatly
denies that allegation.
Aristotle was silent about
this supposed practice of
ostriches.

    Doctor's
orders.

    Pliny, the great Roman
writer spoke about the big
bird's wonderful digestive
system. Other writers
completely refute this
so-called "fact" about the
birds, but many say that
they eat stones.

Break out
the
antacids.

For
dessert,
maybe.

DRUIDS' EGG

    The "authority" for
this interesting belief is
a man named Gough who writes
about it in his 1789
publication. He uses the
term "Druid Glass Rings."
(They are not "eggs", as
such.)
    These rings are

(CONTINUED) supposedly produced by snakes joining their heads together and hissing, which forms a kind of bubble like a ring about the head of one of them.

Reptilian Do-it-yourself.

The rest of the snakes keep hissing, and blow on the bubble until it comes off at the tale of one of them. It then immediately hardens and becomes a glass ring usually about half as wide as a finger ring but much thicker.

A writhing chorus.

Unique tourist souvenir.

Green is the usual color though some are blue and some have wavy streaks of white, blue and red. There is some speculation that snake stones as they were also called were used as charms or amulets among the Druids of Britain on the same occasion as the snake eggs among the Gaulish Druids.

Nice selling points.

Hence the reference to "Druids."

UNDER PILLOW WEDDING CAKE
AND OTHER CUSTOMS: ANNOTATED

MORE UNBELIEVABLE BELIEFS

Some of these beliefs concerned laws. A writer named Barrington comments in his "Observations on our Ancient Statutes" that it was illegal to open a coal mine, kill a crow, or to shoot a gun within five miles of London. This last law may have to do with a statute of Henry VII, who wanted people to use crossbows.

Newcastle competitors?

Hand gun or artillery?

Another law was supposed to force the owners of donkeys to crop their (the donkey's) ears so that the length of them won't frighten horses they may meet on the road.

Horseshoers sideline.

Another supposed law stated that if a man wanted to marry a woman who was heavily in debt, and takes her from the hands of a clergyman wearing only a

Credit cards in those days?

UNDER PILLOW WEDDING CAKE
AND OTHER CUSTOMS: ANNOTATED

(CONTINUED)dress,(the woman),
he, the man, would not be
liable for her debts.

That's all?

Who pays,
then?

Another belief involved
the hare: this animal
supposedly is a male creature
for a full year and then after
that it becomes a female for
a full year.

Matchmakers
dilemma.

Wolves were also in the
doubtful picture: If a wolf
and a man meet and the wolf
sees the man first, the man
will be struck dumb.

Hopefully
not dumb
enough to
stay near
the wolf.

The "Gentleman's
Magazine" for 1771 made these
formal, serious,
straightforward,and confident
assertions: The scorpion does
not sting itself when
surrounded by fire, and the
tarantula is not poisonous.

Too busy
running
away.

Concerning tarantulas,
music has no particular
effect on a person bitten by
one any more than on any one

Forget the
music; get
a bandage.

(CONTINUED)bitten by a wasp.
The lizard is not friendly to
man, and cannot be expected
to awaken a sleeping human
being if a serpent is
advancing on the person.

> That's
> _real_
> unfriend-
> liness.
> Sleeping
> near
> snakes?

A remora (a fish that
attaches itself to other fish
with a sucker) doesn't have
the power to retard the
sailing of a ship by
attaching itself to the
bottom of the vessel.Spiders
like to fix their webs on
Irish Oak and do not hate
toads.

> Don't
> even
> try.

> No reason
> to hate
> toads

THE MILLER'S THUMB

One of Chaucer's poems
describes a miller as having
a "Thumb of Gold." A writer
named Sampson mentions the
phrase "The Miller's Thumbe"
in his 1636 publication.

> Good
> adverti-
> sing
> slogan.

Different Writers tried
to determine the meaning of

(CONTINUED) this term; some have said that it meant that the miller was honest. Others said that the term "Miller's Thumb" actually referred to what was called the strickel, a device used in measuring corn. It leveled the corn, probably when it was being dispensed.

MEDIEVAL HIGH CONSU-MER SATISFACTION RATING SEAL.

According to speculation it might have had a rim of gold to show it was standard, honest, true, and not fraudulent.

No federal Weights and Measurement Departments

In Randle Holme's Academy of Armory and Blazon (1688) he writes: "The Strickler is a thing that goes along with the Measure, which is a straight Board with a Staff fixed in the side, to draw over Corn in measuring, so that it doesn't exceed the height of the measure."

What does armor have to do with corn?

Definitely not "AS SEEN ON TV"

"800" to call for any problems?

UNDER PILLOW WEDDING CAKE
AND OTHER CUSTOMS: ANNOTATED

"TO PLUCK A CROW WITH ONE"

This is a saying with certain variations that was popular in the sixteenth and seventeenth centuries. One of the variations was by a writer named Dekker in his publication dated 1630.

Plucking chickens would be easier.

Heywood, in 1598, wrote "We have a crow to pull." The meaning concerned a jealous wife whose husband was taking certain liberties with her maid.

Animal abuse?

Wives were the last to know.

None of the writers seemed to go into details as to exactly what those liberties were. There is a corresponding expression in Howell's "Proverbs" (1659): "I have a goose to pluck with you, or I have something to complain about."

Ask the smiling maid.

The goose might also have some complaints

TO BEAR THE BELL

Years ago a bell was a common prize according to a

UNDER PILLOW WEDDING CAKE
AND OTHER CUSTOMS: ANNOTATED

(CONTINUED)writer in the
"Gentleman's Magazine." He
wrote that the reward of
victory in 1607 at the races
near York (England) was a
little golden bell.

What, no
roses?
How did they
figure the
odds?

Later the following
sayings developed from that
situation: "To bear the bell"
or "To bear away the bell"
meant success of any kind in
any endeaver.

Especially
ding-a-ling
ideas.

BULL-RUNNING

This was a popular
sport celebrated annually
many years ago at Stamford
in Lincolnshire (England.)
A description of this
activity was described in a
publication entitled the
"Butcher's Survey of the
Town" dated 1717.

Something
similar in
Spain.

The butchers of the
town provided the wildest
bulls they could find and

UNDER PILLOW WEDDING CAKE
AND OTHER CUSTOMS: ANNOTATED

(CONTINUED) the animals spent
the night before the run in
the stable belonging to the
Alderman. The next morning
a proclamation was made that
all shops and stores along
the street of the run be
closed. The proclamation
also said that absolutely
no violence was to be done
to strangers that happen to
be in town during the
bull-running.

Political
pull.

Not
exactly an
ideal day
for
shopping.

Good
Public
Relations
from the
Chamber of
Commerce.

A guard was appointed
to assure the safety of all
travelers and strangers.
After the aforementioned
proclamation, the town gates
were shut and the bulls
released from the Alderman's
stable.

Men, women, children
and dogs immediately
pursued the bulls carrying
Bull-Clubs which were used

UNDER PILLOW WEDDING CAKE
AND OTHER CUSTOMS: ANNOTATED

(CONTINUED) to spatter dirt in each others (peoples') faces. William Earl of Warren, the first lord of the town stood upon his castle walls in Stamford watching the bull-running activities.

To confuse the bulls?

No binoculars in those days.

He reported that he saw two bulls fighting for one cow. A butcher of the town, the owner of one of those bulls, had a great Mastiff dog with him, and he accidently set his dog upon his own bull.

Watch it, boys. You're supposed to be running, not romancing.

"Don't you recognize me?"

That bull joined in the general running followed by other large and small dogs; the chasing, noise, and tumult drove the bull crazy and he started running in all directions along with the other bulls.

"We'll give them a show for their money"

The noise was so great

(CONTINUED) that William heard the din in his castle; he then mounted his horse and rode into town to see what was going on. He actually was very amused by the racket, noise and confusion of people, dogs and bulls running all over town.

"This is my town, and I'm proud of it!"

He was so delighted by everything that he gave the meadow in which the two bulls were found fighting to the butchers of the town in which to keep their cattle. There was a condition, however: it was that the butchers have to provide at least one lively, mad, and crazed bull for every bull-running in the future.

A nice present from the Boss.

Keep the tourists coming.

ANCIENT FOOTBALL

Every year in Scotland

UNDER PILLOW WEDDING CAKE
AND OTHER CUSTOMS: ANNOTATED

(CONTINUED) long time ago at a certain time the batchelors and married men would line up opposite in a field. A ball was thrown out and they played from two in the afternoon until sunset.

What about time outs?

A player would get the ball and run with it until he was overtaken by a player from the opposite team. The ball-carriers opponent would grab him, the ball-carrier, and if he could shake himself loose while holding the ball, he could keep running with the ball.

Centered?

Hey, referees: HOLDING!

Was passing allowed?

If the ball-carrier was actually seized he would throw the ball away, unles it was taken away from him by one of the other opponents. No one was allowed to kick the ball. The object of the game for

We now say sacked.

Forget punting.

(CONTINUED) the married men was to throw the ball three times into a hole in the ground. The object of the game for the batchelors was to dip the ball three times into a deep place in the river.

Easier than touchdowns or field goals.

Not too deep.

The team that could do what it was supposed to do (first?) won the game. If neither team won, the ball was cut into equal parts at sunset.

Then what do we do with it?

According to reports there was always some scene of violence between the teams. Every man in the area was obliged to turn out and cheer and support the side to which he belonged; if he neglected to do this he was fined.

Lots of flags down.

Be a fan or else.

LADY OF THE LAMB

At Kiddington in

UNDER PILLOW WEDDING CAKE
AND OTHER CUSTOMS: ANNOTATED

(CONTINUED) Oxfordshire (England) anciently a fat, live lamb was obtained for an interesting ceremony. The women of the town had their thumbs tied behind them, after which they would all run after the animal.

Sack race variation

The woman who was able to grab and hold the lamb with her mouth and teeth was declared "Lady of the Lamb." The animal was then dressed with the skin hanging on, and then carried on a pole in front of the winner and her companions to an open area called "The Green."

Hopefully there was a dentist on call.

Formal, of course.

Was her name "Mary?"

A party followed with music, a Morisco dance of men and another dance of women. The next day the lamb was partly baked, boiled, and roasted for the "Lady's Feast" where the

Thumbs up for the winner.

UNDER PILLOW WEDDING CAKE
AND OTHER CUSTOMS: ANNOTATED

(CONTINUED)"Lady of the Lamb" sat majestically at the upper end of the table with her attendants.

Wearing ermine or lamb's wool?

TOASTS

Going back to ancient Roman times, the men used to drink as many glasses in toasts to their several mistresses as their were letters in their names. In the publication called "The Laws of Drinking" (1617), the concept of toast drinking called "In order" and "Out of order" was put forth.

Girls with long names line up.

Best seller?

Drinking "In order" meant that people imbibed strictly according to the way they were sitting. Drinking "Out of order" meant when the drinking went on any which way regardless of how and where

Alcoholic chairs.

UNDER PILLOW WEDDING CAKE
AND OTHER CUSTOMS: ANNOTATED

(CONTINUED)people were
sitting; this routine also
meant that drinkers could
down two cups at a time.
According to "The Tatler"
publication, the word
"toast" in terms of drinking
originated in an incident at
Bath (England) in the reign
of Charles II.

    On a public day a
gorgeous and beautiful girl
was in one of the baths.
As could be expected, a
crowd of admiring men
watched her and one of the
more ardent guys drank a
glass of water in which the
girl was bathing.

    He then drank her
health to the crowd.
Not to be outdone, another
man getting very excited
offered to jump in the bath
alongside the girl; he

"I like
thish
method
better"

For
strictly
therapeutic
reasons.

Passion has
no bounds.

A truly
unique toast.

UNDER PILLOW WEDDING CAKE
AND OTHER CUSTOMS: ANNOTATED

(CONTINUED) didn't like the
"beverage" (bath water) of
the toast, but he was

Backscrubbing fun, at least.

determined to participate
in the honor. The rest of
the men talked him out of
doing this and convinced
him that the best rule to
follow was "look but don't
join the bathing."

Or touch the customers.

SCOTCH AND ENGLISH

This was a game played
by children on the border of
England and Scotland before

Juvenile patriotism

the union of the two
kingdoms. A writer named
Hutton described this
activity in his "History of
the Roman Wall" (1804).

The village lads on
each side of the border
formed groups and selected
from their number two

By voting or drawing lots?

captains to lead each group.
Both groups would then take

(CONTINUED)off their coats and pile them in two heaps in their own respective territories; a stone marked the division between the two kingdoms.

What was the weather like?

Each side would then "invade" the others territory and try to get the "enemy's" clothing. There is no details as to what the "invasion" actually involved; it could have been just running back and forth.

Easy scoring.

Not quite like soccer.

If a boy was caught by the "enemy" he became a "prisoner" and could only be released by his own group. There were times when one side took all the boys and coats of the other side.

Political rummage sales.

SHUFFLE-BOARD

Shove-groat, slip-groat, slide-thrift, and shovel-board are some of the

(CONTINUED) ancient names for the modern game of shuffle-board. Sixteenth century writers mentioned all of these names, and it was one of the games prohibited by Statute 33 of Henry VIII.

Eating is more fun than shovel-board.

The shove-groat shilling mentioned in Shakespeare's Second Part of King Henry IV was supposed to have been a piece of polished metal used in the play of shovel-board.

This game was very popular in spite of the royal prohibition and residences of the nobility and mansions of the very rich had them; the great hall of the residence was the usual place for the shovel-board games.

How about cruise ships?

Where the TV goes now.

Some writers mention a

UNDER PILLOW WEDDING CAKE
AND OTHER CUSTOMS: ANNOTATED

(CONTINUED)""shovel-board table" which would imply that the game was played at places other than the floor. Public houses also had shovel-board games.

No darts in those days.

DRUNKARD'S CLOAK

A writer named Gardiner many years ago wrote a publication entitled "England's Grievance" and described an interesing punishment in the time of the Commonwealth.

It related that the Magistrates of a certain town penalized drunkards by making them carry a tub with holes in the sides for the arms to pass through; this was called the "Drunkard's Cloak" and the individual had to wear this through the streets of town.

Probably teetotalers.

Could they still drink while carrying this?

UNDER PILLOW WEDDING CAKE
AND OTHER CUSTOMS: ANNOTATED

SHOES

The custom of throwing an old shoe after a person to whom success is wished goes back many years; shoes are often thrown toward married couples, too.

Successful in dodging thrown shoes?

In Ireland there was an old ceremony of electing a person to a government job by throwing an old shoe over his or her head.

Saved election costs.

A poet named Shenstone opines that the custom of scraping when a person bows may be derived from the ancient practice of casting shoes backwards off the feet.

Just stay in front of the person.

A curious story is related in the Statistical Account of Scotland (Vol X) concerning a King on the Isle of Man who sent his shoes to his Majesty of Dublin. (Probably the Mayor)

Also best personal regards.

UNDER PILLOW WEDDING CAKE
AND OTHER CUSTOMS: ANNOTATED

(CONTINUED)The Isle of Man
King required his Majesty of   A scepter
Dublin to carry them (the   would be
                                     somewhat
shoes) in front of him (his   more
Majesty) when he walked   appropriate.
around in front of his
people during a high festival.

    The Isle of Man King
actually threatened his
Majesty of Dublin if he
didn't follow orders.
Loyal subjects of his Majesty   You'll
of Dublin urged him not to   look like
                                     a
submit to this indignity,   fool.
but he, who was described as
having a rare sense of   Very rare.
humanity, singular wisdom,
and probably with a good   The laughs
                                     on the
sense of humor, went ahead   King.
and did it.

WATCH THE ANIMALS

    In ancient times the
activities of various animals
were studied very closely for
meanings and signs. A

(CONTINUED) publication
called the "Astrologaster"
by a writer named Melton
stated that when a cat
washes its face over its ear
there will be a great deal of
rain.

Feline barometer.

    Considering
precipitation again,
"Nature's Secrets" written
by Willsford says that if a
cat likes the warmth of a
fire more than usual, or
licks its feet, or trims the
hair of its head and
whiskers, rainy weather will
come soon. If bats come out
of their places quickly after
sunset and fly around, fair
and calm weather is
predicted.

Using a comb and scissors?

Out of belfries too?

    It was once believed
that the cry of woodpeckers
meant that rain will come
soon. Buzzards or kites

How about the tapping?

(CONTINUED) soaring extremely high and covering large territories were supposed to presage hot weather. Cranes flying aloft and quietly in the air foreshadowed fair weather, but if they made noise and got lost, a storm was coming.

They could use the thermals.

Global Positioning System (GPS) needed.

If herons flew up and down vertically at night not knowing where to land, "evil" weather was approaching. According to the writer Willsford, bad weather was forcasted if doves came home to their houses later than usual.

Where have you been all night?

If jackdaws came home from looking for food late, cold or "ill" weather was predicted. According to the "Statistical Account of Scotland" (1792), when gulls appear in the fields, a

Long lines at the super market.

- 174 -

(CONTINUED) storm from the
south-east generally
follows, and when the gulls
fly back to the shore, the
storm usually abates.

Meteorol-
ogists
take note.

According to a legend
popular among the peasants
of Ireland, birds once
gathered together to choose
a King of All Birds. They
decided that the title would
be bestowed on the bird that
could fly the highest in the
air.

Avian
Associat-
ion
Convention

A competition of the
feathered creatures took
place and it was assumed by
most of them that the eagle
would prevail, win, and
become King.

Odds-on
favorite.

A tiny wren, however,
had other plans which
included royal ambitions; it
decided to make up with
strategy which it lacked in

Little
birdie,
big
ideas.

(CONTINUED) size and strength.
As the eagle made
preparations for its high
altitude flight, the wren
jumped upon the eagle's back
and hung on as the great
bird took off.

> Check altimeter, submit flight plan. Oxygen.

The eagle didn't feel
anything because the wren
weighed very little. The
great bird flew higher and
higher and soon was above any
of its rivals. The little
wren hung on its back, but
the eagle still didn't know
it was there.

> Aerial birdie-back.

The eagle flew to the
point where he knew he was as
high as he could go and was
positive he would win; just
before he was about to start
his descent, the wren jumped
off his back and flew even
higher than the eagle. He
jumped back on the eagle's

> His "ceiling".

> The height of birdie determina-tion.

- 176 -

(CONTINUED) back for the
ride down. The birds on the
"Crown the King of All Birds
Committee" didn't exactly
know what happened but it was
clear to them that the little   Not even
wren flew the highest, higher   a
even than the eagle. The   photo-
                                       finish.
Committee then proclaimed the   Ermine
wren as being the "King of   and a
                                       tiny
All Birds."   crown.

ELECTION DAY
MONDAY OCTOBER 1st, 1804

This was the day that
certain elected officials
including sheriffs were
presented to the people with
a great deal of pomp,   Rallies
                                       too, of
parades, and ceremony.   course.
It started with the lord
mayor and aldermen proceeding   Political
from Guildhall and the two   differen-
                                       ces
sheriffs with their entourage   already.
from Stationers Hall.

UNDER PILLOW WEDDING CAKE
AND OTHER CUSTOMS: ANNOTATED

(CONTINUED) Each group embarked on the Thames River, with his lordship the mayor in the city barge and the sheriffs in the Stationers' barge. From there they all went to Palace Yard, and then to the Court of the Exchequer.

Which route had the Casino?

After the usual salutations from the bench with the cursitor baron presiding, the recorder presented the two sheriffs. The several writs (mandatory precepts issued by a court) were then read and the sheriffs and senior undersheriffs took the usual oath.

"View with alarm and point with pride."

"Hear ye, hear ye"

The tenants of a manor in Shropshire then come forward to introduce themselves at which time the senior alderman below the

UNDER PILLOW WEDDING CAKE
AND OTHER CUSTOMS: ANNOTATED

(CONTINUED) chair steps
forward and chops a single
wooden stick. This is a
symbolic gesture and a token
of its having been customary
for the tenants of that
manor to supply their lord
with fuel.

Meaning
what? Get
your own
wood now,
your
lordship?

After that, the owners
of a forge in a nearby
parish introduce themselves,
and an officer of the court
in the presence of the
senior alderman produces six
horse shoes and sixty-one
hobnails (a large headed
nail for boot-soles.)

Busy
three-
shift
forge.

The horse shoes and
hobnails are counted in
front of the cursitor baron
who on this particular
occasion is the immediate
representative of the
sovereign.

Diversif-
ication
reasons,
maybe;
industry
as well as
farming?

Every one then embarks

UNDER PILLOW WEDDING CAKE
AND OTHER CUSTOMS: ANNOTATED

(CONTINUED) on their
respective barges and
returns to Blackfriars-bridge
where the state carriages are
waiting. Then they all
proceed to Stationers' Hall,
where a most elegant
entertainment is given by Mr.
Sheriff Domville.

No wild
parties,
of course.

An article published in
a magazine sometime befor
in 1790 described some other
interesting election rites.
On the election of a bailiff
(an under-officer of a
sheriff), the inhabitants of
a community assemble in the
principal streets to throw
cabbage stalks at each other.

Kinder and
gentler
than
bricks.

The town-house bell
gives the signal for the
beginning of this vigorous
activity, and the time period
is called the "lawless hour."
After the cabbage throwing

Was
throwing
cabbage
stalks a
crime?

(CONTINUED) sessions which
did last an hour, the
bailiff elect and his staff
in their robes , preceded by
drums and fifes,visit the
old bailiff, constables, and
other dignitaries.

They hopefully didn't get hit by a cabbage stalk.

While doing this they
are attended by the mob. In
the meantime the most
respectable families in the
neighborhood are invited to
meet and fling apples at the
bailiff and his group of
assistants and friends.

Better aim with apples?

BIG PARTY NIGHT

At a certain night of
the year in England many
years ago, farmers, friends
and servants get together at
about six o'clock.

Y'all come.

They then walk out to a
wheat field and light a
number of small fires and one
large one.

UNDER PILLOW WEDDING CAKE
AND OTHER CUSTOMS: ANNOTATED

(CONTINUED) The servants, headed by the master of the family, pledge the group in old cider and everybody drinks plenty of the delicious liquid. All the people then form a circle and every one starts to yell, shout, shriek, and scream;the same type of noise and shouting is heard from adjacent farms, villages, and fields from various distances.

Better than new cider.

A county rather than a community "sing."

Sometimes thirty or forty of these fires can be seen from miles around.After all this loud merrymaking, the people go home where the housewife and the maids prepare a delicious supper.

Including drinks to soothe the vocal cords.

A large cake has been baked which looks like any other cake except that it has a hole in the middle.

Better re-read that recipe.

UNDER PILLOW WEDDING CAKE
AND OTHER CUSTOMS: ANNOTATED

(CONTINUED)After supper every one troops out with the bailiff (keeper of the oxen) to the Wain-house where oxen are kept. A rite and ceremony is performed.

The bailiff's a human being,not another ox.

The master of the household stands in front of the assembled group and fills a large cup with strong ale. He then stands near and opposite the first and finest of the oxen.

Forget the cider.

He pledges the animal in a curious and of course, oxen type of toast; the other people follow the master's example by toasting all the other oxen and calling each by name.

The personal touch.

After this the large cake is brought in and with much ceremony put on the horn of the first ox through the hole in the baked item.

UNDER PILLOW WEDDING CAKE
AND OTHER CUSTOMS: ANNOTATED

(CONTINUED) The ox is then tickled vigorously in a ticklish area of its large body. This must be done in an effective way in order to produce the proper results.

By a Professional Oxen Tickler (P.O.T.) of course.

The animal is tickled to make it toss its head; if, when doing this, it throws the cake behind it, the lady of the house gets the baked goody. If the cake is tossed in front of the ox, the bailiff gets it.

No prompting, please.

All the people then return to the house to find the doors locked; after they sing merry and happy songs the doors are opened. After they come in the party really starts which lasts into the late hours of the night.

The right keys did it.

Were the oxen invited?

All the people including the servants drink a glass to

(CONTINUED)their master's
health and to a future
bountiful harvest and then go
home. There they continue the   Non-stop
feasting and eat cakes made   party.
of caraway seed soaked in   Rum
cider; they feel that this is   soaking
                                    is
their just reward for their   tastier.
past work on the farm and in
other areas.

PANCAKES

In the "Gentleman's
Magazine" for 1790, a writer
states that at a certain time
of the year the Under Clerk   A fairly
of one of the schools enters   high
                                    official.
one of the school buildings
preceded by various
school officers.

The Clerk then throws a
large pancake over the bar   Flying
(a separating device) which   flapjack.
divides the upper from the
under school. A man who was
formerly one of the masters

UNDER PILLOW WEDDING CAKE
AND OTHER CUSTOMS: ANNOTATED

(CONTINUED)of that school
told a different story: he
said that the clerk threw a
large pancake over the
curtain which separted the
sections of the upper from
those of the under
scholars.

New school course: Pancake Throwing 101.

    According to a report
dated 1560, the boys at
another school were allowed
to play from eight o'clock
for the whole day; after
that the cook   would come and
fasten a pancake to a crow
(the bird, a female.) This
would be done while the
young birds are coming to
the female with the pancake.

Yippee..no classes!

Latest birdie designer fashion.

Mama, I'm hungry.

Butter and syrup?

THE CUSHION DANCE AT WEDDINGS

    This dance is begun by
a single man who takes a
cushion in his hand and
dances around the room to

A girl would be more fun.

(CONTINUED)music. When the music stops, he stops and sings a song with the following words: "I'm not going to do any more dancing."

Tired?

The musician says: "Why not?" The man: "Because Mary Brown won't dance with me." The music starts again. The man: "She must come and dance with me whether she wants to or not."

Play the field and find another woman.

Assertive is the word.

The man then puts the cushion down in front of a woman on which she kneels; he kisses her singing: "Welcome, Mary Brown!" Both of them dance and sing together.

A pleasant change of mind.

Then the woman takes a cushion, stops singing, and says: "I'm not going to do any more dancing." The musician says: "Why not?"

UNDER PILLOW WEDDING CAKE
AND OTHER CUSTOMS: ANNOTATED

(CONTINUED) The woman: "Because John Brown won't dance with me." The music starts again. The woman: "He must come and dance with me whether he wants to or not."

Good girl, now it's your turn.

The woman then puts the cushion down in front of a man on which he kneels, saluting her; she sings "Welcome, John Brown" and they both hold hands and dance around.

She'd rather be kissed.

Next, the whole group is taken into the dance ring and they all sing: "Farewell John Brown." Then they all go out of the room one by one as they came in.

John probably left long time ago.

The women are kissed by all the men in the group as they all go out, and likewise all the men are kissed by all the women.

Don't go yet..this is getting interesting.

UNDER PILLOW WEDDING CAKE
AND OTHER CUSTOMS:..ANNOTATED

GOOD TIMES AT WEDDINGS

A publication dated 1543 describes the following wedding: A great deal of activity and excitement takes place after the feast and banquet.

Now the fun really starts.

The bride herself is the "star" and center of all the merrymaking and excitement. She is brought into an open area in front of all the guests and her clothes are carefully examined.

Prepare yourself, girlie.

According to the publication, this "examination" is not just a cursory and hasty check from a distance; it is rather a detailed, careful, very close, and possibly even intimate procedure.

Is the groom watching or was he lured into another room?

The material, the sewing, the fit, and any ornaments are carefully

UNDER PILLOW WEDDING CAKE
AND OTHER CUSTOMS: ANNOTATED

(CONTINUED) and closely
noted. Very closely. The
girl's anatomy is also taken
into consideration with
regard to the fit of her
clothes.

> Also very
> carefully
> noted.

   They're not through
with the bride yet. After
submitting to the detailed
clothes examination, she is
expected to dance with any
man who asks her even though
he is rude, drunk,
unmannerly, or even uncouth.
She cannot refuse.

> Enough is
> enough.

THE MARITAL QUESTION

   An ancient story is
told about the girl who is
about to get married. She
asks her mother a question:
"When the wedding and dinner
and festivities are over
should I immediately go to
bed?"

> Pre-marital
> advice.

- 190 -

(CONTINUED) Her mother answers:"No, you must dine first."The girl asks another question:"And then can I go to bed?"Mother:"No you must dance first."

What about the groom's opinion?

Girl:"And then can I go to bed?"Mother:"No, you must go to supper first." This question and answer duel supposedly goes on and on, but the girl finally, after the wedding, gets to go to bed.

Loosen and limber up.

"I already ate, Ma. I want to do something else."

QUINTIN

The word quintin, also called quintain, is mentioned in many ancient writings concerning marriage sports and games. One version of the activity concerns a quintin defined as a buttress, a thick plank of wood set deep in the ground of a highway.

A definition of marriage?

(CONTINUED) This is in an area where the bride and groom are to pass. The young men mount their horses and carrying poles run a tilt trying to break their poles presumably against the quintin. The man that breaks the most poles wins a prize which is a garland of flowers.

On their honeymoon?

Man/wood jousting.

Gee, thanks but I'd rather have a trophy.

Another type of quintin activity involved something actually called a machine. It was a post stuck in the ground with a swiveled cross-piece mounted horizontally on it.

In a wide sense of the word.

The cross-piece is broad on one end and pierced full of holes. A bag of sand is hung on the other end and it swings around if its moved with any blow.

To let the wind through.

The action of the sport

UNDER PILLOW WEDDING CAKE
AND OTHER CUSTOMS: ANNOTATED

(CONTINUED)was for a youth
on horseback to run toward
the broad part of the
cross-piece as fast as
possible and try and hit it.

Watch
that
target.

If he didn't hit the
broad part, the onlookers
would jeer and criticize him;
if he did hit it, the bag
of sand on the other end
would swing around toward
him and be about to hit him
in the neck.

A win-win
lose-lose
situation.

The youth's ability to
avoid this was the test of
the agility of him and his
horse. The ultimate goal of
the sport was for a player
to actually break the board
(the quintin, cross-piece)
and he who did it was the
grand winner of the day's
sport.

Apprentice
jockey
training.

No flowers
please.

UNDER PILLOW WEDDING CAKE
AND OTHER CUSTOMS: ANNOTATED

WEDDINGS, MARRIAGES, AND SOCKS

An ancient wedding belief involved the girls in a family. The saying was that if the youngest daughter in a family should be married before her older sisters, they, the sisters, must dance at her wedding without wearing shoes.

Mommy's and Daddy's little girl.

Call for the fumigator.

In a Boulster Lecture dated 1640, a time-honored wedding custom was described: During the ceremony, the sole of the bridegroom's shoe was laid upon the bride's head. This was supposed to signify with what subjection she should serve her husband.

Gently, very gently, please.

The bride might have other thoughts.

Stockings were used many years ago in England as part of a curious wedding custom. This involved the bride's stockings taken by

UNDER PILLOW WEDDING CAKE
AND OTHER CUSTOMS: ANNOTATED

(CONTINUED) the young men and the bridegroom's stockings taken by the girls. This group sat at the foot of a bed and threw the stockings over their respective heads.

Fair exchange.

Real cozy bed game.

The point and the positioning of this activity was to cause the stockings to fall on the bride or the groom. If the bridegroom's stockings, thrown by the girls, fell on the bridegroom's head, it was a sign of their, the girls, speedy marriage.

Field goal.

"Order my wedding gown"

If the bride's stockings, thrown by the men, fell on the bride's head, it was a sign of their, the men's, speedy. marriage.

"Order my tux."

UNDER PILLOW WEDDING CAKE
AND OTHER CUSTOMS: ANNOTATED

SACK-POSSET

Years ago in the evening of the wedding day before all the company left, sack-posset was eaten and the bride and groom would taste it first.

Security measure.

Sack-posset was a food made of milk, yolks of eggs, wine, sugar, cinnamon, nutmeg, and other non-stipulated ingredients. Eating this concoction was an ancient custom of English matrons: they believed that sack-posset would make a man lusty, with the sugar ingredient making him kind.

No listings of all ingredients in those days.

Experience is the best teacher.

More sack-posset was brought to the married couple the next morning. The authority for this information was a publication called the "Fifteen Comforts of Marriage."

Bring some more; the matrons were right.

What are the other fourteen?

UNDER PILLOW WEDDING CAKE
AND OTHER CUSTOMS: ANNOTATED

BRIDE PLACEMENT

A British publication dated 1711 posed the following question: "Why according to custom is a bride placed in bed next to the left hand of her husband when the man gives his right hand to his wife when they go out walking together?" The somewhat puzzling answer was: "Because it looks more modest for a lady to accept the honor her husband does her as an act of generosity at his hands, than to take it as her right, since the bride goes to bed first."

Who cares as long as she's there.

A bride in bed; a wife when they walk.

That's what's important: so she can warm the sheets.

THE HIGHGATE OATH

This "Oath" was administered to travellers at the Red Lion Inn. The guest, called the "party proponent," was sworn on a

Welcome and start swearing.

UNDER PILLOW WEDDING CAKE
AND OTHER CUSTOMS: ANNOTATED

(CONTINUED) pair of animal horns fixed on a pole. The "Oath" was as follows: to swear not to eat brown bread when he could get white bread; not to drink small (weak) beer when he could get strong beer; and not to kiss the maid when he could kiss the mistress.

Extremely serious choices.

Which is the prettiest?

There was, however, what was called a "saving clause":"unless you like it best" for each of the preceding oaths. He was also told: "But so you don't lose a good opportunity, you may kiss them both."(The maid and the mistress.)

A way out.

The best part of the oath.

Other choices were that he could kiss the horns or a pretty girl if he saw one which would presumably absolve him of the Highgate Oath.

Forget the oath, just give me the girl.

UNDER PILLOW WEDDING CAKE
AND OTHER CUSTOMS: ANNOTATED

NEW YEARS DAY WINDS

In a paper published in Scotland in 1794, an authority wrote that certain weather predictions could be made based on atmospheric conditions on the first night of January.(January first.)

The claim was made that the direction from which the wind blew on that night was an indication of the weather for the rest of the year. If the wind blew from the west, it was called the night of fecundation (fertility, productiveness) of the trees.

Long range almanac.

Arborists delight.

The name of that night in the Gaelic language was "dar-na-coille." If the wind blew from the south, it meant heat and growth; if it blew from the west the meaning was fish in the sea

Farmers take note.

Double meaning. (Trees.)

(CONTINUED) and much milk.
Cold and storm was predicted Hoist the
if the wind blew from the warning signals.
north. A wind from the east
was supposed to mean much
fruit on the trees.

HASTY PUDDING

Sir Henry Piers, in his
Description of Westmeath,
1682, described an
interesting Irish custom.
This custom was that every
May Day, which they
considered the first day of A little too soon.
summer, they would enjoy one
formal dish in addition to
anything else they may eat.

This food was called
stir-about or hasty pudding. Gourmets and gourmands take note.
The ingredients were simple:
flour and milk, boiled
thick.

This dish was
considered a good example of

UNDER PILLOW WEDDING CAKE
AND OTHER CUSTOMS: ANNOTATED

(CONTINUED) a good and
excellent wife's cooking.
She was considered a fine
wife because she planned the
food supply well enough to
have the aforementioned dish
for May Day.

Stashed
away
plenty
of
milk
and flour.

Her planning was good
so that food was adequate
for the rest of the year
until the harvest when there
would be plenty of milk,
butter, cheese and curds.

Not easy
with
no
refrigera-
tion.

The stir-about or hasty
pudding was such a
traditional dish, however,
that it was eaten all year
long even in wealthy homes
where there was plenty of
other kinds of foods.

Fillet
Mignon
side
dish.

FISH STORY?

A man named Martin
wrote about the Western
Islands of Scotland in 1716,

(CONTINUED) and the Isle of Lewis in particular. There was an ancient custom there of sending a man to cross the Barvas River every first day of May.

North of Scottish mainland.

Bridge, boat or ferry?

His function was to prevent any females from crossing the river first; if that happened, the people said, the salmon would be hindered from coming into the river all year around. This custom was supposed to have its source from a foreign sailor many years past.

An interesting mad race to the river.

There goes the fishing.

HAWTHORNE FLOWERS

An old custom in Suffolk, England involved the servants "earning" something they liked very much. They were told that if they would bring in a branch

Tips, maybe?

(CONTINUED) of hawthorne
(a thorny shrub of the rose
family) in full blossom on
the first day of May, they
would be rewarded with a
dish of cream for breakfast.

Wow! Round dish special.

Later on the custom was
abandoned not so much
because the masters didn't
want to give the reward, but
because it was difficult to
find the white-thorn in
flower at that time of the
year.

Botanical con game.

MATCHMAKING

An unmarried woman who
happened to be fasting on a
certain day of the year was
advised to go through a
certain procedure if she
wanted a husband.

Frugality is a virtue.

She was told she should
put a clean tablecloth on a
table and put food on it.

UNDER PILLOW WEDDING CAKE
AND OTHER CUSTOMS: ANNOTATED

(CONTINUED) The food should consist of bread, cheese and ale; after that she should sit down at the table as if she was going to eat. She had previously left the door open.

A T-bone steak would also help.

Maybe also a look of marital hunger.

According to custom, the man whom she will marry in the future will come through the door.

He will pour some of the ale into a glass, drink to her, and bow; after that he will refill the glass, leave it on the table, bow again, and leave.

Enough bowing already, let's get acquainted.

GANGING DAY

According to a London newspaper dated October 18, 1787, a large number of men would get together in the fields and one of the more aggressive

(CONTINUED)men is designated
as the leader. As the leader
the rest of the men must
follow him wherever he goes
up hill and down hill,
through ditches, into ruts
and over rough and rocky
ground.

ATL..
All
Terrain
Leader.

    If they meet any people
along the way, men or women,
two of them are "bumped."
This means that two of the
young men in the leader's
group grab the arms of two
of the people they meet and
swing them against each
other.

A real
honor.

Handshak-
ing
is
passe'.

    Most of the women of
the area stay at home during
this period of jollity, but
some do venture out so they
can drink the ale and eat
the plum-cake that home
owners give to the
merrymakers. If the weather

The brave,
hungry,
and
thirsty
ones.

(CONTINUED) is nice these
females spend the best part
of the night in the fields;
according to tradition
that's where they are
supposed to enjoy all the
delicious goodies.

Bring more
ale
and
plum-cake.

LEEKS

Leeks are a biennial
bulbous plant allied to the
onion and also related to
garlic, shallots, and
chives. The are also the
national emblem of Wales and
have their place in British
history.

Pungent
relatives.

A publication dated
1678 called the "Festa
Anglo-Romana" stated that
Britons wear a leek on
March 1 celebrating a
famous battle and victory
over the Saxons.

Like later
military
ribbons.

During the fight the

(CONTINUED) Britons
wore leeks in their hats
which were their military
colors; the vegetable also
served to identify the
soldiers so they could   Weren't
distinguish between their   the
                                   uniforms
fellow battlers and the   different?
enemy.

    Reference to leeks
goes back even farther than
that to A. D. 633, when the
Britons were fighting under
their King Cadwallo at
Hatfield Crace in Yorkshire.
The battle took place near a   Aromatic
field full of the vegetable.   inspira-
                                  tion.
The date of 1658
also mentions the following:
"The Welchmen, in
commemoration of the Great
Fight by the Black Prince of
Wales, do wear leeks as   Proudly.
their chosen ensign."

UNDER PILLOW WEDDING CAKE
AND OTHER CUSTOMS: ANNOTATED

GOOSE AND GEESE

Goose was a popular dish in England in the autumn of the year at the end of September. One of the reasons given for this fact is that geese were plentiful at that time. Roast goose was eaten then, and it was also the day when tenants paid their quarterly rent to the landowners.

Hazardous too, maybe?

A story about Queen Elizabeth concerns the eating of goose on a certain day in 1588. She was having dinner with one of her subjects, and after eating goose she raised her hand in a toast to the following: "The complete destruction of the Spanish Armada."

Did Bess pick up the tab?

Hope springs eternal.

As soon as she finished the last word of the toast she got news of the defeat of

(CONTINUED) that naval
force. According to reports,
ever afterwards on that day
of the year she ate goose in
commemoration of the Armada
defeat.

Memo to
the Royal
Kitchen.

There was a popular
saying and proverb in those
days to the effect that if a
person eats goose on that
particular day, he or she
won't go hungry for the next
year.

Fine, but
please: No
more goose
on plates.

In Denmark during
harvest time, every family
had a roasted goose for
supper on a certain evening.
Ploughmen also ate and
enjoyed goose at harvest
home.

A honking
good
time.

A holiday fair, called
a Goose Fair, was held at
Nottingham in England at the
beginning of October. It was
called that because of the

UNDER PILLOW WEDDING CAKE
AND OTHER CUSTOMS: ANNOTATED

(CONTINUED) large quantity of geese that were slaughtered and eaten. A father brought his three sons to this fair and he had raised them totally secluded from the outside world, especially and completely from women. The reason for this is not known. They had never seen a member of the female sex.

Castle tower

They didn't know what they had been missing.

When they reached manhood, their father took them to the Goose Fair and he, their father, promised to buy each of them what he wanted.

Fatherly treat.

They walked around the fair and the sons asked the names of everything they saw. AS they strolled around they came upon some very beautiful women working.

Hot dog? Carmel corn? Cotton Candy? Ferris wheel?

The boys looked eagerly and intensely at the lovely

UNDER PILLOW WEDDING CAKE
AND OTHER CUSTOMS: ANNOTATED

(CONTINUED) females,wondering
and marvelling at these
strange, stunning creatures.
They asked their father what
they were. Papa had to think
fast and said to his boys:
"Those silly things are
geese." All the boys then
instantly said: "Father, buy
me a goose."

Pretty,
but what
are they?

You're
holding
back on us,
Pa.

They
grew up
fast.

THE HOBBY HORSE

A hobby horse is a type
of child's toy composed
usually of a stick with a
horse's head on the end.It is
"ridden" by the individual
who puts his or her legs
around the stick.

Simple,
but
effective.

Self-
propelled.

In ancient times it was
related to the Morris
Dancers and considered much
more than just a child's
toy. A writer named Tollet
considered the hobby horse

(CONTINUED)to be a decorated
and fancy "King of the May."
He described it as having a
golden bit, a purple bridle,
and a golden tassel studded
with gold.

The man riding the
hobby horse was no less
elaborate, with a purple
mantle trimmed with a golden   Circus
border latticed with purple;   and parade
a purple crown; and a purple   livery.
cap topped with a red
feather.

The individual "riding"
the thing also did tricks of   The start of
legerdemain (magic) and   vaudeville?
engaged in mimicry. The horse
itself was sometimes made of
paste-board and colored a
reddish-white similar to
peach blossoms. Something
was suspended from the
horse's mouth to collect
donations from spectators.

UNDER PILLOW WEDDING CAKE
AND OTHER CUSTOMS: ANNOTATED

BRIID'S BED

A publication called
"Description of the Western
Islands" (1716) by a writer
named Martin mentions an
interesting ancient custom
observed on the second of
February.

The mistress of a family
along with her servants take
a sheaf of oats and dress it
up in women's apparel. They
then put it in a large basket
and lay a wooden club nearby;
this they call "Briid's Bed."

After that the mistress
and her servants yell out
together: "Briid is come!"
"Briid is welcome!" They do
this just before going to bed
and when they rise in the
morning they look among the
ashes (of the fireplace),
expecting to see the
impression of Briid's club

Designer
clothing
of
course.
Security
reasons.
Who?

Still not
identified.

How did
that
happen?

- 213 -

UNDER PILLOW WEDDING CAKE
AND OTHER CUSTOMS: ANNOTATED

(CONTINUED) there. If they
see that immpression it means
that they will have a good
crop and a prosperous year.

Rural,
rustic
almanac.

SPANISH INCIDENT

A writer named Seward
wrote a publication entitled
"Anecdotes of Some
Distinguished Persons," and
an interesting incident
involved King Charles V. He
was travelling through Spain
and passed through a village.

Like
Kings.

As he walked along he
saw a peasant approaching him
from a distance. The man's
headwear looked odd and as he
approached the King, he, the
King, noticed that the man
was wearing a tin crown on
his head.

About to
make
obeisance?

A royal
convention
in town?

He was also holding
something in his hand,
possibly something that may

- 214 -

(CONTINUED) have looked like a scepter. As the man came close to the King, he, the peasant, ordered the King to take off his (the King's) hat to honor him (the peasant.)

Slight role mixup.

His majesty, completely in possession of his regal dignity, said to the man: "My good friend I wish you joy of your new office. You will find it a very troublesome one, I assure you."

You will get nice perks.

I (the King) will take my bonus.

PUDDING PIES

Young people in Kent, England celebrated and enjoyed the holiday season by eating pudding-pies in public houses. Thia activity was called, strangely enough, pudding-pieing.

Maybe they had to say this fast while eating.

The size of these

(CONTINUED) goodies ranged
widely from the dimensions
of a teacup to that of a   Immense.
small tea-saucer. They were   Even bigger.
flat, like pastry-cooks'
cheescakes with a raised
crust to hold a small
quantity of custard. Currants   Choice of
were lightly sprinkled on   flavors?
the surface.

    People had to drink
something along with the   Crop
pudding-pies, of course, and   rotation:
the ideal beverage was   hops to
                                  trees.
cherry-beer. Coach
travellers going down the   No pits,
                                  of course.
road towards Canterbury were
often greeted with these   Cherry-beer
refreshments from inns along   too, of
                                  courshe.
the way; they were invited
to taste the pudding-pies.

STONES AND DOUGH-NUTS

    Boys will be boys and
children will be children

UNDER PILLOW WEDDING CAKE
AND OTHER CUSTOMS: ANNOTATED

(CONTINUED)even during
ancient   times. An author
named Heath wrote about the
Scilly Islands (a group in
the Atlantic Ocean off the
coast of Cornwall, England)
and described a unique
custom of boys.

To say
the least.

    At a certain time of
the year they threw stones
at night against the doors
of peoples' houses. The boys
claimed that this practice
was a privilege from time
immemorial and they
considered it nothing less
than a sport.

Good
exercise
for
pitching
arms.
Spare the
windows,
please.

Was there
a stone
throwing
league?

    The author was unable
to find the source for this
practice, but wrote that he
was told that the same
custom was followed in
several provinces of Spain.
It was also followed in some
parts of Cornwall. If the

Olé.

UNDER PILLOW WEDDING CAKE
AND OTHER CUSTOMS: ANNOTATED

(CONTINUED) boys were told to stop doing this, they made certain demands to cease: pancakes or money.

We eat or line our pockets.

The kiddies at Baldock, in Hertfordshire in England also had their fun on a certain day of the year. That day was designated Dough-nut Day. Small cakes fried in hog's lard were placed over the fire in a brass skillet and served to the delighted children.

No holes?

The beginning of dunking?

MAY DAY CUSTOMS III

A man named Andrew Clark, who was Official Printer to the Honourable City of London published the "Laws of the Market" in 1677. A section in this treatise was called "The Statutes of the Streets of This City Against Noysances".

Executive Type.

(CONINUED)(Annoyances.)This statute forbad men to go around the streets of London either by day or by night holding a bow in the bent position.

Robin Hood, take note.

They were also not allowed to carry arrows; wear an unscabbared sword; or carry a hand-gun with powder and match. If any or these edicts were violated, the penalty was imprisonment.

Walking ammo dumps.

However all of the foregoing was allowed if the man was engaged in some kind of a game concerning the holiday of May Day.

Question: What kind of game or games were played?

NEW YEARS EVE II

A writer wrote about an interesting game played on the Western Islands (The Hebrides,)off the west coast

UNDER PILLOW WEDDING CAKE
AND OTHER CUSTOMS: ANNOTATED

(CONTINUED)of Scotland.)On
New Years Eve at the large
impressive abode of the
Laird, a large number of
people would gather.

Auld
Lang
Syne.

   One of the men would
dress himself in a cow's
hide after which other men
beat him with sticks. He
then frantically ran around
the hall making loud noises
while the other people ran
out of the place making
believe they were extremely
frightened.

Hopefully,
small sticks.

Like
"Help!"

   After the people leave
the hall and go outside, the
door is shut. Being outdoors
in the Hebrides on New Years
Eve is not exactly a great
pleasure and the guests want
to get back into the castle
as soon as possible.

Chilly,
too.

   They try to get back
in, but they have to repeat

(CONTINUED) a certain verse to do so; word, however, soon gets around regarding that verse and they get back into the castle. The writer didn't know the origin of this game, nor did he know what finally happened to the man wearing the cow's hide.

Shivver until the "password" is said.

The tanner is looking for him.

UNDER PILLOW WEDDING CAKE
AND OTHER CUSTOMS: ANNOTATED

GENERAL INDEX

Ale...........................129
All Fools Day/April Fools
                    Day.......127
Allhallow Even(Halloween)......36
Amusing Trench.................135
Ancient Football..............161
Ancient Love..................116
Ancient Pastimes...............96
Ancient Sports and Games.......16
Archery.......................108

Bar The School Doors...........42
Barley Break..................112
To Bear the Bell..............157
Big Party Night...............181
Boxing........................103
Bride Placement...............197
Briid's Bed...................213
Buckler-Play..................107
Bull-Running..................158

Carnival Time.................142
Cat and Dog...................105
Christmas Customs..............88
Christmas Pies.................91
Cushion Dance at Weddings.....186

Dark Lanterns.................149
Drinking Customs...............44
Druids' Egg...................151
Drunkard's Cloak..............170

UNDER PILLOW WEDDING CAKE
AND OTHER CUSTOMS: ANNOTATED

Election Day
    Monday October 1st, 1804.177

Fairs......................60
Farming and Agriculture.....69
Farming Charms.............118
The Feast of Sheep Shearing.77
Fish Story.................201
Fool Plough................143
Fun With Sailors...........137

Ganging Day................204
Golf.......................110
Good Times at Weddings.....189
Goose and Geese............208

Hasty Pudding..............200
Hawthorne Flowers..........202
Hob or Nob..................54
The Hobby Horse............211

"King Arthur"..............139

Lady of the Lamb...........163
Leeks......................206
Loggats....................113
Lord of Misrule.............92

UNDER PILLOW WEDDING CAKE
AND OTHER CUSTOMS: ANNOTATED

The Marital Question.........190
Marriage and Betrothing
                Customs.......1
Matchmaking...................203
May Day Customs I..............27
May Day Customs II............29
May Day Customs III...........218
May Poles......................30
The Miller's Thumb...........155
The Montem....................38
The Moon......................78
Morris Dancers...............33
Mumming (Maskers).............85
Music.........................125

New Years Day..................23
New Years Day Winds..........199
New years Eve I...............22
New Years Eve II.............219

The Highgate Oath.............197
Onions Will Tell.............123
Ostriches....................150

A Prize of Bacon.............140
Pall Mall....................114
Pancakes.....................185
Playing Cards.................59
"To Pluck a Crow With One"....157
Presents for a Gentleman's
                Gentleman....136
Pudding Pies.................215

UNDER PILLOW WEDDING CAKE
AND OTHER CUSTOMS: ANNOTATED

Quintin........................191

Royal Oak Day..................81

Sack-Posset....................196
Scotch and English.............167
Shoes..........................171
Shuffle-Board..................168
Spanish Incident...............214
Stones and Dough-Nuts..........216
Sword Dance....................130

Tavern Signs...................56
Toasts.........................165

Unbelievable Beliefs...........147
More Unbelievable Beliefs......153
Under the Rose.................52

Valentines Day.................26

Watch the Animals..............172
Water Custom...................84
Weather Omens..................132
Weddings, Marriages, and Socks.194